surrealism du jour of a woman-child unbound:

disorienting tales to enchant and perplex

by Delicate Bellwether

First paperback edition April 2021

ISBN 9798735198635 (paperback)

Prologue

This woman-child is at the least young adult,
daughter, sister, and mother, all-in-one. She whirled
into being. Whether she became embodied at the
behest of someone or of her own volition is
anybody's guess. Delicate has a surrealist goal to
create absurdist prose bizarre and imaginative,
while still and all relatively fathomable. Her writing
makes sense to a limited extent, but is meted out
with scant detail. The effect is that these fanciful
tales evoke familiarity the more they're read.

Full of herself, Ms. Bellwether will at
intervals confuse, astound, disgust, and delight you.
Through experiences rife with the banal, horrific,
magical realism, or sci-fi with its bending of space-
time itself, the stories will endear themselves to
you. So come along with her for the ride of your
life. The travelling is fine. Don't miss out.

<u>*Contents*</u>

Week 1 - Day 1 - Part 1 - Mittie's Mean Feat

Chapter 1

Upon taking a spoonful of rice pudding, Mittie Oglevy muttered a shocked oath, "Dammit to hell!" She'd noticed forlornly that a HAIR was in her mouth! She retrieved the long, loopy thing, still clinging tenaciously to bits of rice, butter, and cream suspended, along with the single slimy hair, in a pudding. "Where did THIS come from, outer space?!" Mittie roared. She smiled smugly to herself at how clever this phraseology was. What she didn't know was that she, Mittie Oglevy, was onto something. The hair had come from outer space. To be entirely accurate, it had come from an exoplanet in an alternate universe, but this fact was amazingly close to her surmise.

An entire hair having been transported is no mean feat. As an added improbability, it'd belonged to a being with the name Mittie Oglevy as well, who lived contentedly in that alternate universe.

The Mittie on earth was reasonably content, too. She created mischief on the daily, pointed out others' errors in convos, and generally delighted herself with how delightful she found herself. She lapsed momentarily into an uncommon reverie wherein she received top honors for being an allround near perfect human. Along with the pudding, Mittie lingered over her b-day card from her mum with the annual b'day cheque for £10. Mum had given £1 per year until she'd reached 10 years, when she'd levelled off. That'd been 39 years ago.

She squinted at her blurry visage in the mirror across the room, pleased at the familiar lopsided grin she typically sported. At that precise moment she heard a wrapping on the door. The wrapping made a penetrating rapping, causing her to shift her gaze. A gaudy holiday gift sack was now stuck onto the inside panel of the front door and had definitely not been there when she'd passed the door going to the kitchen. The sight of the thing perplexed her. She was the only one home.

She flung open the front door to find Kris there, with the Kris namepin stuck on the breast of their t-shirt like always. Kris was her bestie. For the life of her, Mittie didn't know what their age nor sex was, nor for that matter did Kris even know Kris's gender identity exactly. It seemed immaterial to the pair. What was also unbeknownst to Mittie however, was that this was a version of Kris from an alternate universe that, as is arguably predictable by now, was not the same universe where the other Mittie had lost a hair in her pudding.

This substitute Kris demanded to know where Mittie had been, just as the earth Kris might have, had they not been mute. "You weren't there, like you said you'd be." Kris pronounced 'weren't' as '**wur** uhnt' in a surprisingly calm, yet squeaky, voice. Mittie taught grammar school by trade. Over Summer Recess, she and Kris had gotten along famously sans conversing, pinching apples from neighbors' lawns, scouting deep into the nearby wood, examining snake eggs (or were they tortoise?), and swapping neighbors' mail around in postboxes. It was clear from this activity that Kris could adequately read addresses and numbers. It'd all been loads of laughs, to the point that Mittie had taken to leaving a note on the front door of Kris's nearby flat the night before with the time and place to meet next.

"I was distracted, was all," said Mittie unconcernedly. She knit her eyebrows again then, adding, "Since when did you start to speak, by the way?" Kris couldn't settle down and started striking a fist into the opposite palm. "All right, then," Mittie continued obligingly. "Ramp it!" This term that she'd dreamt up was rather opaque code for "Take it up a notch!" Kris crouched a bit, a cross between an unwieldy, stocky toddler and a sumo wrestler, and lunged at Mittie's shins, knocking her off balance. The two feel through the floor in a freefall state. Though their eyes stayed open, they rubbed frantically at them in an attempt to see clearly.

Their worldview had gone all misty, as if fog were building up on a camera lense. Implausibly, they groped their way onto soft pillowy matter the size of beanbag chairs with the feel of rubbery dough, devoid stickiness. Though out of focus, the large shapes appeared to shine faintly through the gloom. Their grey hues were etched with silver tracings and lacked discernible edges. By detecting how undeniably slowly they themselves were descending and accounting for the minutes ticking on toward an hour, one point became unmistakable. If either of them missed the next clump as it arose from below, they would without a doubt fall very far down! They'd undoubtedly covered a great distance already. The clods of matter rose up, buffeting them, or 'trapping' them, between pillows. So the two slowly worked their way down the fragments as the fragments went up. They felt with their hands conscientiously for the next, which reliably rose up to greet them. This floaty, heady development was altogether the most relaxing, yet simultaneously invigorating, experience either had experienced.

After what was around an hour but seemed an eternity, the clumps changed. Now they were prickly, almost like an odd mix of rough sandpaper and holly leaves; they smelt burnt, and they were in fact very hot and getting hotter by the instant. Kris squeezed through some to maneuver into a tight space next to Mittie. The two instinctively turned to face one another, for there were fewer nerves on their backsides.

"I think I'd rather have gone to the pool than this," Mittie admitted.

Kris, to the surprise of both of them, said humbly, "Sorry for tackling you. I'm not sure what came over me."

They felt with their feet and ankles now for the next fiery clouds, or whatever they were, to arise. After two to three more horrific earth minutes, all movement ceased, and the shapes were gone. They found that backless, metal rolling stools with spongy, black, round cushions had positioned themselves under their bottoms and they sat, suspended in apparent nothingness.

Chapter 2

"I'm not the person you may think I am," said Kris then.

"I know," admitted Mittie hesitantly. "I've never asked about that, only because I wasn't quite sure how to broach the sub ...."

"No," Kris cut in. "It's not that. Of course you didn't know about that. Nobody does. I mean to say, and listen intently to me, Mittie, I am NOT THE PERSON you think I am. I'm not THAT KRIS. I just know their business, even if I've never met them." Kris waited a bit, to let this sink in.

"So, you're a different Kris-type person-type?" Mittie paused for a long, long beat to consider this.

She then went on, "In that case, would you mind telling me if the earth Kris is a girl or a …"

"Stop." Kris II put in. "This isn't the time. Plus how would I know if that is something I should even be divulging to you? Trust me, I've seen some stuff where I'm from, but it looks like we're in an especially fine kettle of fish." Interestingly, flying fish had started leaping about them mid sentence and now continued when Kris trailed off, their lacy pairs of pectoral fins coming quite close to them, causing much batting of eyes and arms.

Mittie asked, somewhat exasperatedly, "Will you at least tell me if YOU'RE a boy or a girl?"

"Sure, no sweat. I'm a …"

Chapter 3

A rope ladder unfurled from above with a blast so deafening, Mittie wasn't sure whether Kris II had finished the sentence or not! Between them, the ladder dangled an absurdly out-of-place holiday wrapping identical to the one on Mittie's front door, seemingly a lifetime ago. It was one of the newfangled paper gift bags with flimsy handles, but this one had a special matching tag.

To: Mittie and Kris II
From: Climb up, and you'll see

Mittie touched the tag, and it disintegrated to ash. The bag was flapping in a sudden wind as severe as all get-out. She chanced a glance inside the tote and, despite the fluttery flapping, found 2 preposterously heavy bottled energy drinks. How the bag withstood this weight as it flung wildly about was beyond her, but she gave Kris II a 500 millilitre and cracked open the other. It tasted of smooth caramel. Fortunately, she was adroit at climbing one-handed up rope ladders in strong wind gusts, so she took the lead.

Book 2 - from Mittie's perspective

I saw loads of people eating loads of foods. They must've been on holiday to be eating the feast that lay before them. We crawled over tables so fast, it was extremely difficult, nay impossible, to try to avoid the me'lange of dishes. Clearly, we were getting a knee into someone's plate here and the heel of a palm into a gravy boat there. Yet the uncomprehendingly quiet paucity of murmurs was just as oppressive as the shrill loudness of so much silverware clattering on plates. All in all, it was insufferable. People took no pleasure, apparently, in the well laid spread, chewing and swallowing with the haunted look of ones depressed beyond measure. I didn't know why we must hurry so; but I just knew we must! We scurried hurriedly onward.

Above the 49th table, a huge clown head bobbed. Apparently alive, it screeched, "Glad you were able. Sit at table!"

A couple of child clowns appeared, rolling on metal
stools, rolling our metal stools before them. We ate
until we were stuffed. Grape leaves with rice,
tomato with tuna, cabbage leaf with beef, hollowed
bell pepper with blood sausage. I'd never tasted
meat, so I was unsure if it was real. I had seen these
dishes prepared on t.v. When I bit my tongue, it
bled profusely. "The mouth heals quickly," said
Kris II, with a wink. I thought with a jolt I could
nearly make out dozens of all-but-translucent
roaches swarming our table for an instant. It was
then young kids came in.

Walking very close together in a long line, they
came unaccompanied and unbidden, single file.
Touching one another, unmasked, naive, eyes
shining, nothing did they ask. The clown head
loomed and grinned, gap-toothed. "You teach them
NOW!" it screamed. "Reading, writing, 'rithematic;
never falter - that's the trick!"

"But I'm unprepared to die!" I cried, eliciting a
seismic sigh.

Kris II piped up, "Don't be ridiculous. There's no
use making a fuss. You're unprepared to keep them
safe. You've not prepared their lesson. Just do the
best you can, Mittie. They're eager little beavers."

We two stood abruptly up and sang fingerplays.
Kids knelt on haunches, and they knew quite a few;
Eensy Teensy, Where is MiddleMan?, Little Cabin

in the Wood. One got hurt as they stood up from the ground. He couldn't stop shaking as he howled and howled. "Hold your hand above your heart, and don't shake your hand so," I remarked soothingly. Touched, I might've been tempted to hug him, but the clown head loomed and had a go.

"No more intercession! Come to inner sanctum!" Eyebrows raised, we made our way … up a plastic staircase. Inside was a bounce house with a thousand coloured balls. The children stooped to remove their shoes. To approach the speed of light, I'd heard, you hold your mouth just right. We didn't reach the speed of light, quite; but our ship was glowing red to anyone watching from behind. Inside we all were weightless, bouncing crazy, on our heads.

At long last, frenzy gave way to exhaustion, and all but the most dedicated gave over to sleep. The craft halted immediately without the least tug of a jerk, and I alone had donned a parachute and a sharp pair of strap-on crampons. It appeared skydiving and scrambling on escarpments were in my future.

The last panorama I saw, as I readied to tumble out backwards, was a miniature version of the Kris II I'd found and yet another youngster. Little Kris and "tiny Mittie" were waving 'bye' to me. I'll never know which ones they were, or even if they were real. I don't know if I'm real now, as I climb back onto the soft, puttied clouds. Nor do I know if the sun will have set by the time I get back to my land.

I'm sturdier, though, with renewed hope inside that I'll sprint right up this clandestine cloudcase before it becomes molten lava that will scratch me, besides.

Intrigue!

There was a girl in our carpool, and it was her b'day. A boy was at an event with a team on a bus. Dad told me to tell this boy he has to get back on time. Busses were almost always late.

This girl named Rita, whose birthday it was, had to get a package to a top administrator (male) at the private school. I had to deliver it. Something didn't seem right about it. I slit the seal and cut the package open. There was a damning letter in the parcel meant for a bad kid who went there - or it may have had a double purpose to trigger action from the head man. By removing it - what would implications be? Danger!

Wrappings

Driving down a road, we saw a family of children outside wrapping gifts. Then we saw loose wrapping paper had blown away, then 2 rolls of it further; we went across the street to the car park where there were nice squares of shiny wrapping paper still folded.

We went to see friends at a flat, but it seemed like a hospital. Bright, white halls. One of our friends, Leslie, was very sick, as well as her significant other who was still in bed. We went into his room to see if he needed anything. We told them about the wrapping paper. It was theirs. We left to get some food, though they had chili on the stove.

The paper was gone. Dozens of bicyclists were racing all over, toward us, as we tried to go back.

At a restaurant, an older couple ate with a friend they'd traveled with each year. She -
much younger - had a new boyfriend, black-headed, with long hair. He had a wild tic - bobbed his head constantly - talked loudly, cracking silly, insane wisecracks. He offered a gripless hand to shake. The subject of their annual trip came up. The newcomer was all in! Resignation and dread filled them as this realization settled on the couple and the new girlfriend.

Vaccinations

I had one shot in my arm and went to the next clinic to wait. But before going straight there, I went to a restaurant with women friends of my mother's age. One pulled another's bra cup off in the restaurant, but there was no breast there. "It looked like an ear", they said. It looked more like a big, cutout, baked biscuit to me.

The plumbing was out. It was so bad, the water drain didn't even go into the output spout to empty. Backed up. Not usable.

I went back to the original clinic to make sure I should travel to a third one. The patients were all gone. There were still a few women workers, extremely stressed, but nice. I saw the main doc - male. I got the Okay to go on to the 3rd clinic, not back to the 2nd one.

Rituals, pure and mundane

You could take swathes of white lace to perform rituals without diminishing their holy properties. We therefore did so, taking every precaution, at a hotel. There could be mud on the towels, but that could be shaken off and vacuumed later. One had to take care to get only a very small fingerful of the necessary accompanying clear fluid. It would quickly diminish and evaporate out into the atmosphere, leaving the lace in its pure state for the religious to use for their purposes.

We did just that. Management lent us the hotel vacuum sweeper.

Others, including friends of mine, had so very many sacks of food in another doss-house near the supermarket. These men worked long and hard on their project from the room, their headquarters. But one with whom I'd not made an acquaintance was the considerate soul who'd shown / shared with me the secret of these bags of sustenance. They had pretty nutritious vegetables in them, at times. But more often than not, they just held sugar-laden sweets, mostly made up of carbs.

Remote findings

Clay Daugherty and I worked hard at this. There were copies of actual books and a catalogue indexing them. These were not the same books, though. We could go through and order new science resources for each grade level at our school. Money was appropriated.

In a house that doubled as a private school. … There was a skeleton. The woman had written names sloppily on green sticky notes and was calling out names of the students who needed to get something turned in. The kids must've been there, or it was remote. - Weird, long names. I looked back at them - it was impossible to read them, but she lived there and was their teacher.

A car was pulling in and skidded. We thought it was Zeke's, but it was grey and small. It turned a little, with the brakes or gears making a grating noise, and then went on. I knew I had a long trip to go on. I

found a quantity of wine, and I drank it anyway,
telling myself, *"It'll be okay."* I found a very wide
ring - it'd been left / lost. It was "mine", I decided.
But it was too big around and still had a type of
price tag on it. It was so wide, it was like a corset.

Fall, Climb, Tenuousness

I fell backward off the rooftop on the couch with 3
others. We touched a tree. Meg didn't help grab. I
did. We had green arms, but broke our fall. In USA.

Later we climbed up to get in a church - freezing.
Had to pull myself up and over the ledge and in -
hundreds of men with long white beards - levelled
seating. Hard to get in. My legs froze. So many
were behind, waiting.

Curry Long Talk went up around construction
workers working on earthen stairs. I'd have to audit
classes that I'd miss the 1st day. Meg taught, I
think. Something happened - collapse! I couldn't go
back down! (My existence had never been more
tenuous.)

Smell Chasing

I was in a big mall. Some young kids were fighting
but an analysis showed which one actually hit
harder on the x-ray. (It appeared in slow motion.)

I came to a seat way up high and sat in it. It was
suspended high up in the air by a chain or a hook.
Someone below, a man, said, "just sit in it". This I
did, and it took off like a ride chasing a smell in
Hyperspace Mountain. I went through many rooms,
up and down, and it was seeking a tiny, scented
mist. I got back to the start of the ride. Some female
workers said I'd have to find an outfit and a hair
curler (roller) that were missing. I tried to complain,
but I couldn't. Two young kids worked there, too,
sons of the 1 sensible man. I went back and found
part of the outfit.
A restaurant was next to the ride. The workers at the
fast food establishment had a shirt with TRY on it.
Female people were answering the phone, taking
orders. I heard, "Just call 999". I realised what
they'd said. I said, "You can't!"
They said, "Well, we do."
It was messing with the system. I mentioned it to
the man who ran the ride, and he said, "<u>I</u> know." At
least he believed me, but was helpless to change it.

BRIGHT WHITE FLASH

I was looking for a place and stopped my car too close to the train tracks. There was a loud sound, the arm coming down. I had to back up. I tried to push something on the dash. BRIGHT WHITE FLASH - blinded me!! I was OUT!! I came to and tried explaining to the people in the car behind me. "It was not my button to turn on the (emergency) flashers!!" I'd gotten turned around, so I went back up the road a little ways.

I saw many kids in the distance playing at a colourful outdoor playground in a housing estate. I stopped to look around, as I was still lost. A young woman was climbing up to her flat by literally climbing the outside of the building. She was very scantily clad, so I could see her big body, visible from below, but couldn't see the clothing from my perspective. I went back up the motorway and made it to a major intersection. I turned right.

Since I was unsure where to go, I stopped at a deserted bar and went inside to ask the way. The man who owned the building was there and showed me on his huge computer with multiple screens how the bar had been built. The panels appeared to converge. These panels, representing the walls of the bar, were like green-leafed trees with clouds and blue sky behind them as they came together. Then he showed me (video of) the first skit that had been enacted there with almost no narration. The set was like a Western, and there was a trapdoor.

Many kids came boisterously in, and among them was a little girl of about 8 years of age. She was a former student of mine, but hadn't attended my school for several years, as she'd moved away. We were wild with delight! She had been a crazy kid, but was so glad to see me! I picked her up in our ecstatic embrace!

"Free samples" and pit stop

All fast food restaurants had a special on this day. Basically so cheap as to be free. My significant other ordered dozens of long veggies with big, white, bulbous heads and limp, long bodies and a <u>lot</u> of other foods. I went to work on this, my first day there, for more or less a 10 - hour stretch. It took many hours for the order to come out - we were so far behind. I got the order eventually and took it home on a break. It had (uncooked) spaghetti in the package with it, too.

At the store, there were little "free samples" (packs of uncooked spaghetti).

A child was at the house where I took my break. I didn't have time to eat. Cristie Minkin had been dating a wild man who seemed rough, always in black, and acted mean and bad. It turned out it was all an act. She was with him 'forever', and then I'd seen her at the store without him. They'd broken up.

She wasn't happy, but was covering up any
emotion.

I took a shower and was trying to get some of the
food back up off of the floor quickly before I
dressed to go back to work. Cristie M's ex was
pushing a mower outside the bathroom window. He
mowed right toward me. I tried shielding my
nipples with my hand as I bent over to get food that
had dropped beside the toilet, but it had several long
wet, light grey turds on it. I had to pick this feces up
with my fingers and fling it back into the toilet. I
think I accidentally revealed my bosom.

Back at work, I met the manager. He was very nice,
and I had been working for around 10 hrs. without a
break.

My husband's phone got a message for me to check
my phone. A man said I did need to go ahead and
rent a flat after all for a family who would be
coming to the U.K. Later, this occurred again, but
this time he checked to see that I'd done it. I had.

There was loud noise outside, and I saw a crane lift
a car and hoist it into a pit that had just been carved
out of the ground. A front-end loader was refilling
it, the pit. I went out and yelled above the roar -
"What are you doing?" He stopped, but indicated he
would continue. So I went to the back door of the
house to alert the owners. One old woman was
cooking. Another came out and saw that it looked
bad and went back to try to get the other one's

attention. The older, cooking woman told me off
and closed the door! ?

Cinema

I taught high school. I was in the library. We had
the upper floor. Kids were assigned to come as a
small class. I tried to make it interesting. They
weren't too bad, as I think they sensed my panic
and felt sorry for me. Some of the girls gave me
advice. Another female librarian worked there, too.
After class, while we waited in the lobby for classes
to change, an audio was lesson piped in. It was on
whether it is okay to plagiarize. I said, "NO," very
loudly. In the lesson example, the person had been
tempted and had gone along with it. Quite shocking,
it was! I found out that I had another class in 5
minutes. Panic ensued again.

I was driving to get a snack on my break. A lot of
cars and large lorries were coming in the road
toward me! One steer got loose, ran through them,
and tried to goar something. A man was trying to
get him.

When I got back to work, there were a lot of large,
square, flat boxes being loaded into the back of a
truck by a mum standing back there. She stood on
the truck's elevated platform. One box was party
foods, and some pink things that looked like huge
sticktights got out and fell on me, into my shirt, on
my right breast, and embedded! - Someone with a

saw tried to quickly help me. The saw touched both my cheeks and bits of gravelly glass went in under my skin. It felt crunchy, crumbly.

(There were hundreds of kids wandering halls.)

Now women were there for a convention. I found Bibi, and she said I should go home. She got the list I'd been given for the women to start working on. Very involved. You had to pretest all of them. Depending on results, they would have different assignments. They all came in at once, and Evie and Jake Hester's wife were there. They saw I was hurt / didn't say a word.

I left the room and was going to leave. A handsome man in the hallway was very worried-looking. Another man he worked with was there, and a pretty woman stopped to talk to him. She smiled at me. I asked if she'd worked at Bartlett College. No. Harper Publishing Co.? She said, "Yes". So had the men, I think. A knowing look passed between them.

I didn't know if I could drive. It was as if I was very drunk/drugged. I guessed from the effects of the accident. I sent a message home (to mum) and left.

———

The next day, there were so many foods at a holiday office party. I almost ate one of the mats. All the foods were colourful and beautiful, unrecognizable.

Kids in long queues - looking hungry.

At a cinema was an endearing character, a friend of mine, Smithson, who everyone knew and loved. People would go out to get refreshments often, and they moved around to sit with other people.

I finally decided to go to the WC when a woman was cleaning the theatre, even though the show hadn't ended. She took some others and me in her car and came within a few feet of my car that was parked near an exit. I said "Oh, can I get out here? There's my car!"

She said, "OK," but drove toward the main exit. I got out angrily and walked back to my car. I went to another film at our church. The same older man (Smithson) and many of the same others were also there. An older man - Elton - and a man around my age. We were young.

There was a small seating section of 2 loveseats in a V. There was 1 homemade pizza. I saw pepperoni and perhaps ground beef on it in the shape of a picture. The pieces were huge, the size of paper plates. I asked a woman what kind it was. This woman, who'd made it, didn't know. I didn't want to hurt her feelings by not eating at least a little. I asked what was used to make the picture. She didn't know what I meant. I said, "See how it's brown on the house. Maybe something was used to paint it." We got nowhere. I think I took off a crust to eat ... Maybe.

There was a contest to get to go to the top of The Shard of Glass. You needed 100 votes. A large white tracker like a thermometer was on the promo. Only 98 more votes were needed. Much time passed, ... and 98 were still needed.

Mall Flat and Preschool foods

In a Flat. - a woman lives here at times, but a gay man is here now with some friends. There's an adjoining playroom/school for preschoolers. Normally, a teacher comes for the last session, and some kids stay. By stepping out in the hall and peering through the window one room over, I see 3 girls in there talking to each other - no adult.

I ask about this when I go into the flat. They know. Someone didn't come get the kids. "Do they charge for that?" I ask. (£1 per min.?). No big deal. Food had been brought in that was left over from earlier kids. My uncle Earl is here, too, I think. He or some man made sandwiches with tiny, white rings of cheese on them. Long, like subways - cut into quarters. They added a lot more rings, all over the outside, and falling onto the platter. We could have it if we wanted.
Sunna had told me I **had** to go shopping! Great deals ... I didn't eat. Was to go out into the mall - also part of the flat. I went to shops and looked in but didn't know of these supposed special bargains

nor see any clothing befitting my nature, let alone some that would fit my body.

Later, back in the flat, there was fish and what looked like kidneys or liver. The men there said it would all be frozen. I went into the little anteroom, and there was food like cat food on the floor in a dish, and there was animal hair all over the place. It was some more of the kids' snack food - I came back in with it. Cammie was there. I asked after her husband and mum, "What's going on?" She said they were doing all right, but it wasn't a good thing. She'd been working - but for very little. I said I loved her, and the door closed on her as she left, but I thought she'd reciprocated.

The one (woman) who lived here had left the hot water tap full on when she'd left town for the weekend! There was a switch built into the doorframe. I think it was an opener. You got in the doorframe to ride a plank as it slowly unfolded outward. You had to be careful to use it fast, or it would reclose every time.

They put the food left over from the children on a seat of a booth-like table (like one that folds out in a motorhome) in the room that was the kids' preschool. I worried it wouldn't be good by Monday, as I added the "cat food" to the top of it.

Tutee dysfunctional

A boy had many problems - he didn't want to try to learn. I offered to tutor. They brought him to a building early. I had my red rifle there. We just talked. Others came to have practices and games; asked if there were concessions set up. They'd found my gun and set it out in the lobby.

Later there was a big meeting, and I told that I was tutoring. It was a serious topic. I didn't really say who. Then it became apparent - the boy and his parents were in the audience. The dad had a copper-toothed bird, and he had a 2-pack of dead chickens. His wife was leaving town. He wanted me to cook them. I was saying I may need to break one in the 2-pack off and freeze it, or I could cook both but he'd have to eat quickly or freeze one.

The boy saw another kid around his age at our next session. No bad trauma. He was probably going to start regular school.

There was a curved object of wood or plastic. Its end was dull, but it had heft. You could put your foot on it to try to bend it. We were on a bus. There was a driver, several kids, a large brightly dressed older woman, and the kid I'd been tutoring. He didn't look mad but inserted the curved object's head in her sternum or below it. She let him do it, remaining standing. I was standing right next to him. It took a long time. We were waiting for him to kill her. She told him how to readjust it, "a little lower," she said.

2 new jobs

I had a new job at a restaurant. I hadn't been trained, but I started taking orders anyway.

A fellow member of the waitstaff was congenial and helped show me the ropes. Nothing seemed to bother her, not even the fact that it was widely known by the other workers that she'd been sleeping with one co-worker who was much older than she and another, who was around her age, concurrently. She was fun to work with.

I decided to eat there, and the food was good. The checkout system, however, left a lot to be desired. I got in the queue at one cashing out station. An unusually pretty, quiet woman with a very young son who I'd waited on earlier queued up behind me to pay. I now saw two other boys, presumably older sons, come out from the loo to join her. The older of them looked to be in year 6. Though not ugly, he appeared defeated. I did not see a sense of play, play fighting, or any interaction whatsoever between him and his younger brothers. I looked right at him, and my eyes asked, "How are you?" meaning, "How is your school year going? Are you reading anything interesting? If so, what is it?" Though not verbalized, all questions were answered with his blank stare of apathy. It wasn't going well. It seemed not to even "be going".

I realised that the cashier had been waiting for me to pay. I had slowed down the queue.

I passed another oblong counter-island that had two cashiers facing out from the middle on each side. Each of these was extremely backed up.

I had to go to my other new job immediately. I walked out into the night and went down a long road on foot, all downhill. There was an underpass through which the road went. Above it was a huge skyscraper or mountain. Another road intersected there, also running under this gargantuan structure. The light that indicated whether one could drive or walk across the street was not obvious unless you backed up and stood in a certain area to see the colour of the light at a particular angle. I couldn't make it out. Another person, an even younger female than myself, tried to see it, but she, too, could not glimpse the colour. It took a high level of skill that one must develop. I took the position again and inclined my head just right this time. It was mostly lighting up white, but there was a flash of green in the emission. I started across quickly, and she trusted me enough to cross the street at the same time.

At this other job, we were taking job applications. I had very many men in my queue. The first one was nice and had applied earlier, but hadn't had all his credentials with him. They would need to be matched with his other paperwork. I took it and placed it upside down, flagging it to remind me. I took a half dozen other job applicants' documentation and applications.

Then a large envelope came in. It held a single document, apparently a cancelled cheque. I knew this might hold significance, so I excused myself to find a manager who I knew. I explained to this woman that the man who'd turned in his info earlier held a high chance of being a promising employee. I sensed frustration on her part that the man's earlier packet would need to be relocated.

She looked at the address of the account holder printed in a tiny font on the small paper cheque that had come in. It listed a town many hours away from our location. She thought it unlikely anyone would have sought employment this far from their hometown.

a Caravan and a Motorhome

We were in a little caravan/the library. I had 2 classes back-to-back. I was reading aloud, but they weren't the books I really wanted to read. I had an asst. and she tried helping a lot. She grouped pretty good, interesting colourful fiction with corresponding non-fic.

The 2nd class was fairly small - kids looked like middle schoolers. I asked about low #s, and they said "it's raining." Many kids' parents had come and gotten them. I let them pick where to sit. Very cramped space! (There were low shelves banking a small walkway partially taken up by a rocking chair and other furniture.)

I rented a motorhome and invited people to go camping. It was parked outside our house on Skyland. I put things I would need altogether. We had invited about 6 or 8. I was planning to shave my armpits. I'd gotten up and messed around a little. I got in and asked a man there what time it was and he said it was almost 11:00. I couldn't believe it. We left. Jake drove. I asked the guy if others had been there, too. Maybe they would meet us at the site. He was illusive. He watched out the window intently. He saw things through trees he'd not noticed before and was excited about it. He lived 'right through there,' he said. We crossed a small river and it was truly beautiful. I started telling how I'd canoed it once, but Jake quietened me.

At work, a man had not gotten an item he'd ordered from me. It was a small carrier you wear - like a baby carrier. The box it came in was huge. It was in the building in the wrong area. I looked for a custodian. The person putting it together needed a small pair of pliers. We had a pair and the toolkit was out and open, but I guess Evie was using it. She looked over, but didn't say anything. The custodians were married and the man also had administrative duties. I couldn't find him so I went to the swimming pool in the school. Some were swimming. A couple of black h.s. girls were singing. Holding sheets of paper with hand-written words. It was so ethereal and I knew the tune. I joined the line, looked on with the words and sang with them, harmonizing with a high part. There were at least 6 or 8 of them now. They stopped, and they had loved it.

Topless in school and Naked in pool

A lot of female teachers were at a big faculty meeting. We were going to take off our shirts to reveal our bras at our headmistress's direction in a parent-teacher organization meeting the next time we met. Then she took off her shirt - signaling to do so. We all were wearing just our bras. A playful teacher removed her bra, too, and was spinning and flipping it around. It was an uncomfortable white strapless bra. I realised I'd taken off mine, too.

Later, the students had been taught to read by turning over a gold fabric purse-like object and reading from the centre fob to the right margin by pointing just below each word. Then they'd go down. One girl didn't like the method. I asked an administrator (male) if the girl could not do it that way. He said no. I found her and said I thought she could do it the way she liked, but she said it was all right to do it how she'd been taught.

There were so many books to choose from, arranged by ability level and genre. They were huge, as big as cereal boxes and colourful, arranged stacked high on shelves.

Kids needed bookmarks and really wanted brightly coloured ones. I had a few. In my office I found dozens or hundreds more in many colours, spilling out of a box. I worked with boys and girls to try to help them select what they needed and wanted. This was very important.

The students were in a swimming pool. One former student had come and gotten in, too. He was at least in his 20s. He'd left his cell phone and it rang. A business call. I put my head out the window to call. I went out to the pool because he was frolicking naked in the deep end, playing a game, and diving in with other kids. I took them some bookmarks.

A dog was carrying around a human male doll. It was carrying it by the big droopy nose. I was glad it wasn't carrying it by the penis.

Week 2 - Dorm life and gambling food

Our college had to be approved to open. We all had to meet there. 1st day. There were freebies being given out. Books. Tons of SWAG! My grocery-size paper bag burst. I put it in another that was there, a plastic bag. It was burst, too. I folded it all up and it worked. They came and inspected and said we could open. that. day! We had such a large campus. A woman named Fran tried to get a year 2 boy, Snake, to sign up for martial arts. He didn't want to. I showed a move, 1st form & how to stand. Also how to stand in Tai Kwon Do. He laughed, tried it. He would sign up.

I moved into a dorm. A woman brought me a gift - a form of "cheque". "Put it on the bottom step" (of the staircase), I told her. Another brought a pencil with dangles all over the top. colourful, like elastic coiled phone cords. She wanted to give it to me through my window. I was many flights up, but she was tall! I said I didn't know how to open the window yet. She was insistent. I unrolled a crank & a triangular part came open but there was a screen or plastic over it. Somehow she pushed the pencil through. I talked on the phone to my dad. I said someone might hire me. He had to guess. The person was from Bartlett, a prof. He didn't guess, but it was David Dries. Other menfolks were talking about people they knew in common when I went down to eat in the cafe'. They were excited. On the way back up to my room, I stopped. On the bottom stair, a lot of stuff and a "Cheque" like this

Delicate Lynne
Bellwether.

I was at a conference. The woman sitting near me was talking to me a lot. I told her my sister was 10. Then told her that I was 59. She couldn't believe it! (I was <u>that</u> <u>old</u>.) She had kids, couldn't remember one of her girls' names; she was on the road a lot. I told her that my family members were going to hike very far up a special mountain that day in the Urals and she should come. She was hesitant.

We were visiting relatives.

Back at the house, we were readying to go on a long trip toward home. I hadn't eaten all day. One cousin, Dan, went ahead and put a **huge** baking tray in the oven with biscuits and other foods on it. Rob was there. My dad was wanting to take a detour on the way home to visit more relatives. It would be a long way out of the way. We were already going to be on the road all day. He figured we could fly and talked it over quietly with my mum but I wouldn't do it.

There was a restaurant where you could gamble. It was run by a Middle Easterner. It had a history my mum recited to all as if it were a documentary. A place where he'd lived had had yellow dust that got on his clothes and partway up on the buildings' walls, and the camera pans to show why. The desert panorama is all yellow expanse. He founded

something where nothing had been. He'd emigrated
here.The food was good - a cover for the gambling.

Now you could pick a number, & you invariably
won. You could reinvest & keep on doing it. I won
quite a bit but gave it back. I remembered & pointed
out that it's wrong to gamble, according to the
Bible.

You could go there and get in a tiny cubicle by way
of picking that number. It was like a WC & it stunk
very badly. Others waited in adjacent rooms.

Furtiveness

The door opened and this burly man just barged in,
not having knocked & didn't greet me but walked
quickly through the house. He would stop and look
at patches of the wall that had been patched, would
continue downstairs. … I watched warily from a
distance, not wanting to appear too obvious.

He came upon my husband, & the two talked loudly
and gentlemanly enough, if the stranger (to me) did
speak a bit boisterously & vociferously for my
liking. He seemed to have furtive motives, from
what I'd seen.

I left to run an errand for our son.

Loud music from a trumpet section rehearsal blotted
out most anything else, though other instrument

groups continued to play on the football field that was about 30 yards from our school. Of course we also heard this backdrop by necessity & when our students came, they would doubtless have to contend with the distracting volume of the music, too.

We were readying for the day/week, being speciality area teachers. There was not much time. Dr. Daugherty came around and said we would have a mandatory piped in "svc. announcement" and someone asked which class period. He said, "Year 6." I was sitting on a bare mattress on a bed talking with one gym teacher who I knew and a new one.

I made a face at year 6 & said, "I don't really want Year 6," to which they laughed.

One teacher, Dell, said, "well at least you can see on the schedule when each class will rotate to you".

"I think I'm coming down with the sniffles," I said sillily & they pealed with laughter.

I walked around on a car park & found stacks of dropped coins.

We're going to go to Italy with a large group. There's a female Briton who is our tour guide / unofficial ambassador. Before we meet her, we go to a show at a huge event hall. The son is a large, middle-aged man who impersonates her to build excitement for the whole thing. He wears a mustard-coloured pair of slacks & shirt. He grabs onto one of the regularly spaced mic cords that hangs down from a balcony & pulls himself up by that, turns & reveals a wild-looking countenance, long hair loose & face somewhat grotesque.

Afterward, the son is there to introduce her, but it's very matter-of-fact. He is now normal-acting, still in the same outfit, but calm.

Later we go to her place. We are to wash a lot of clothes before we go, including a lot of her clothes. It's hard to gather it all. Much is on top of a hamper, but we finally get started on it. Mum gets the woman's PO Box #. She gives Mum the name & address of an American man in another state who's a contact. I wonder aloud if we need a physical mailing address for her, but, no. The payments go to the man. It's pretty well set.

Rita has a lot of boogers in her nose.

Rit's inlaws are staying at the woman's house & our mum & dad are, too. It's a type of holding place where we wait. Her father-in-law cannot get along with our dad. They bicker constantly. Much of the time these older folks are there while we're not. I tell her maybe that's just how Big Will likes it or at least how he will always be.

The Gov't wanted "our" baby boy! We didn't think they knew of him or of his whereabouts. But they said they would come for me. I had a plan to smuggle him but it was dangerous. I took a "steely" colour, had an identity swap to be my grandmother in name. I had steely pens.

My own relative asked and doubted it would work.

For a while, I deceived them. I had put him in hiding, in with some luggage. At the last minute, I put him in a kitchen cupboard, down low. He was the size & shape of a drinking straw. I could leave him & come back for him. We were living on a large bank of water.

We'd crossed over the water. He was there somehow. Still the fear persisted!

Recruitment Stress, all over again

I was a young recruiter at Bartlett again. We were going to have a presentation or performance at work, & my hair had to look like I was younger. I had very few details. But a formidable man (Dr. Youngster) on our team asked me about this several times. Each time, I said I would not dye my hair nor let him do it for me at work. I thought of putting it in puppy dog ears.

I went to work after having been on the road for a long time. Everyone had new computers, & mine was ratcheted up on a metal clip that came up through my desk so that the computer base was parallel to the desk.

I was going to have to get it down & was trying to find someone to show me how. Everyone was working like crazy. An admin. asst. was not behind like I was. (My ofc. was typically trashed.)

One woman, Angel, needed something that should've been delivered. I had seen it in the front ofc. under a little stand on a worktop. She was delighted to have found it.

Later a woman named Dell couldn't find her cat clock. I told her where it was, & she got it. They were amazed that I'd known & I said, "if you can't find something just ask me."

My hair and ofc. had to be done by around 17:00. Most of us were fairly panic-stricken.

Pool, Pipes, and a preemie

There was a pool of unplumbed depth at the very edge of our property that no one knew of. Danger!

I was not going to be allowed to get to sleep because there were no bedsheets clean, and my husband and I were fighting about that & other matters.

Same night - I went to a historical tourist site where there were many field trips of primary kids ongoing. My name was still listed, but of course I had quit, so it was my replacement. We struggled to find the child they sought, as it was disorganized. I saw an older teacher, Lucina, who was friendly.

Next day - Back at home, a teacher came to visit unannounced & was eating. She came into the bathroom but I needed to go, too, so I came in & went while she washed her hands.

She had a large appliance like a water heater that she said she'd leave there for storage. She didn't know we'd be moving. We saw a car stop, & a tiny ESL kid scrambled in. He had to crawl in - no doors or seats. His pants were coming down a little in back as he crept up and in. We recognized him, but he had gone back in time several years.

At a church, the women who had assisted in the service really bollocksed the storage room up. It was off of the wings & up a floor. There was a welly coated in mud here & another there, tossed about. I peeled the mud off. They'd been wearing galoshes over the wellies.

There was a bit of water. I could look down & see big exposed pipes that went honeycombing down. O O I tried to hit them with drops of water but some missed. I threw the muddied galoshes into them. People sat in an alcove around these open holes reading in comfy chairs, but didn't look up.

I reported on what I'd done & was told that was good.

There was a tiny, new baby that we had at home now. It was perfect, but must've been a preemie. I didn't know what good it was, but did want to take it & show it around to Zeke, it was so pretty.

The problem would be feeding it. I'd heard women could build up a supply of breastmilk, if needed, maybe by expressing it & getting output that way. I didn't know if I was too old, though.

<u>Also, the baby's mouth would be too tiny to latch on!</u>

Brawls in brothels

There were brawls you could be in. Some were deadly. We went to a tavern, & there had been a brawl because the woman was working there, but inside there were many dead bodies. She had taken part in the killings, along with 1 or more other females.

Then we were going to film a battle. You could decide if you wanted to participate or not. Men had long whips with loops on the end. The women's (whips) were shorter, but adequate. They put theirs onto mine on the ground to try to stop mine, being pesky.

You could go to watch a battle, but instead of a movie, it would be real. You knew there would be bloodshed. It was still very sad because the characters knew each other. The deceit and trickery were real, leading up, & it was with a very heavy heart that they killed, with much remorse afterward.

The foods served at the barroom were pretty good.

One could lash the ship to their own (ship) to try to return to port with it. But if their ship was <u>so</u> much smaller, it mightn't work.

When someone was killed, everyone grew very still, & quiet; & it was extremely scary, in addition to being sad. The way to know if it'd happened was the traces of the disembowelment. Sometimes you weren't sure if it would happen or not, but just know
* there was the possibility &
* so that's what you'd signed on for.

No Duty for me

I was at church, and I hadn't brought a mask with me, so I wasn't going in. I saw that my sister, who lived with me, had driven one of our cars there, too. She now sat in it smoking. It was the white car, not the yellow. She was letting the engine run. All of this annoyed me.

I went to the car & asked her about it. People were now streaming into the church, some men holding hands, none wearing masks. I was very surprised & disappointed, since they're all intelligent.

I said I'd go tell them I would not cover my Sunday School (S.S.) duty of watching the babies.

Inside, I told a woman. "OK," she'd said. What could she say? She showed me photos in the fellowship hall of the babies, in case I at least wanted to see them, & she left.

There were a few others sitting & talking, some fellow kids who'd come up with me & some women I knew. Nobody made a deal out of my act of defiance.

I was embarrassed that my clothing (a dress) was the same that I'd worn the day before.

The photos were now huge, the size of t.v. dinners & colourful! I saw there were 2 of each, & they were laminated in a way, very stiff and plasticized on the front. I saw some pix of babies & kids I knew & took 1 of each of those out, but the woman came back & said, "No." I was not to have them.

I bebutted, "but there are 2." It was an open & shut case - no discussion.

Footwear Troubles

I, along with foreigners who hadn't spoken my language, had endured a marathon voyage in which we'd changed aeroplanes more than twice, in addition to travelling by car at times.

Now I was to begin my new life at school, living in a dorm with rich amenities such as you'd find in a posh hotel. There was a hot tub in my suite, and an indoor pool down the hall. Fortunately, I didn't see another soul in the dorm. So it appeared I had not only my own room but also my floor to myself, if not the entire building. This afforded a great relief, though it did add a certain otherworldliness to the situation, as I seemed to be living in a bombed-out postworld reality.

I stopped in at the schools' gift shop. A woman I knew was shopping there. She showed me some sale items she thought I'd like, a small optional study guide and a few trinkets. She said I could use my student discount to buy these, pushing them across the counter toward me. I said I didn't want to buy these. She removed a couple of things from the pile and said, "You can get a good deal on these," pushing the book and another needless thing toward me. I said I was not buying anything. She raised her eyebrows upon seeing how insistent I was. I could tell she was perplexed that I was going to miss out.

I went off campus to pick up some boots for my grown son. I saw that many people were in the stores. I found some light tan boots of good quality, soft leather. Though I thought I knew his size, I was uncertain enough to delay the purchase. I put a pair on hold.

I needed shoes, too. I knew it would be so hard to find a pair for myself that I almost didn't know where to begin. My feet were so small, I'd need the smallest size or else surrender the whole ordeal in advance by seeking a pair of girls' shoes. But I really wanted antiviral shoes that had been made to protect the feet from the coronavirus making its rounds. I didn't think these were made for young girls. I would be sure to be exposed to this virus while at my studies.

I looked in the boot of my car. There was a used pair of men's tall, green waders next to a pretty pair of used women's dress heels. Oh, no! I felt sad when I realised that when we'd been made to go from one terminal to the other on the trip, a young couple who I didn't know had stowed these, their footwear, in my boot. Now they'd never be able to retrieve them again. Not only did we not speak the same language, we didn't know each other's names nor whereabouts.

At one store, there were so many shoes that I felt an inkling of hope. An older man and woman were busily helping customers, fitting shoes to them and the like. But an announcement came over the loudspeaker: "We will close in five minutes."

Seeing that they were both engaged, I left to head up the mall.

I found shoes that had been treated to keep the wearer's feet safe among countless rows of boxes stacked high in a store. But predictably there were none close to my petite size. I saw another woman I knew there. She was also going to pursue the same course I would.

I returned the way I'd come. When I got to the store of the elderly couple, a large family group hovered just outside its entrance. I couldn't tell if they were preparing to enter or had just left. They were readjusting a parasol on the child's pram and that type thing. I saw there were now different customers being served attentively in the store. The 5-minute warning announced over the PA. I shook my head. Maybe they wanted people to feel rushed up so they'd buy more readily, but they'd looked like such kind souls. I left in frustration.

Pairs of things amidst chaos

There was a job fair at a huge building. There were so many coming, & the people genuinely cared. There were wads of clothes that people had left intentionally that you could get. I found a purple shirt with a duck on it, but there was a problem with it, as in its having ripped, I think.

They tried so hard to find me a job - teaching secondary school, working with just 1 kid. I said

"No," to all. They gave me another one that was purple.

It would snow that night!!

We were staying at a house in the country in the Western Region. There was a lot of work to be done! A young girl was staying for a while as her folks were working. She would go out in the woods & find something like a fish or frog & come back in & make a big mess, setting up a habitat, but never cleaning up. My mum didn't get mad at her ever.

I went into the front parlor, & there were at least 4 or 5 pairs of my jeans lying everywhere, & they all needed to be washed. I started on that, but there were also loads of other chores to be done, everywhere you looked. People would stop by, for just a minute (men).

I saw while I was outside in the front garden that there were huge fruits on a tree. Bright orange (big as beach balls: [breadfruit].) I was quickly peeing when I noticed these fruits & then saw they were in 2 smaller trees in the yard, at least.

Two young men were walking up the road, talking & laughing loudly, so I tried to quickly wipe & do up my pants, all the time, saying loudly, "Look at those fruits!" to distract, so they wouldn't see what I'd been doing.

Two or so (fruits) fell down. The men were handsome. They stopped & talked a while.

Back inside, the girl was wanting & trying to help with something, but had only made a bigger mess - getting tools out, I think.

I saw that a young woman with a wide face, big eyes, & soft, short hair had come onto our screened front side porch. She was asking how far we could take her toward home.

I found Mum & asked her. She said to have the woman wait. I went to tell her, & she'd already fallen asleep. She had on jeans & sandals with straps. On one foot someone had written in red below her toes. 'Have a nice day.' Below it, in white that was less obvious on her skin, they'd printed, 'Hi, Mum!' I did a little more stuff, but I was glad to get a chance to take the young woman toward her home because there was something I needed to leave the house for. I fell asleep.

When I awoke, the house was sparkling clean, & several women were there for a luncheon. My mum then entered, & her hair was styled in long curls & was very dark. She was dressed beautifully & smiled. She showed the exquisitely decorated sandwich cake frosted with glacé icing that she'd made.

I asked suddenly about the woman, & Mum said she'd taken her home. I could tell Mum had learned of the pregnancy, & it would be all right.

I went out, & a male volunteer was helping women volunteers at a school zebra crossing. It was dangerous - the cars did not slow down or stop! It was so hot, & the hill we were on was very steep. The man complained, & he said it's like this every time.

There was a rare break in the traffic, & I got across. I went in a healthcare caravan that was empty at present. It was pretty light inside and neat. I needed a bit of paper toweling so I got some.

Multiverse?

We were in a school, walking along a smooth hallway of polished wood, & there was a slight dip in the floor when we stopped. This was where the event happened every time! A girl in that room was the age of the other teens **and** over 100 years old.

We looked in & saw her, & she was pretty & otherwise normal-looking.

A teacher, Christine Minkin, came out to give me a couple of pointers to help her carry out the deception. It was involved. She had special hairpieces nobody else had that maintained the illusion. Quite possibly, the teen changed sex, too.

She acted naturally, so that it would seem hearsay, a mere urban myth.

On the left of her left leg was a vestigial limb that did not appear, but was most certainly there. An incantation summoned the change. It was a long line, seemingly of pottery, followed by a short addition.

Sex mix-ups & a horizontal Zipline

I was headmaster at a primary school. At the dismissal area, there was a child inside with a red soccer jersey with bold white lettering in the form of a plus sign. He was extremely sick or had been injured.

No car came when his name was called over the loudhailer, & there were only 2 or 3 kids left. I was summoned to see if I could help. I knew the child from an earlier school where I'd been previously assigned. I saw right away that the child's family members were indeed not present.

The child's name was called out again. He wasn't enrolled at our school! I had the contact # from before, so I called it. A man, presumably a much older brother or uncle answered and came immediately. The boy was being brought out, but could barely move on his own.

The lad's relative, now a woman, rappelled parallel to the earth extraordinarily fast, past many extremely high banks of cliffs, as if attached to a zipline. We all saw it happen from a distance.

The difference was that she was bundled and lay prone, as if on a dogsled. Her feet flew first.

Alarming: sounds and behaviours

We lived in an expensive penthouse suite with people beside and on floors below us. There was an alarm sounding in the middle of the night, but it was muffled. My father & I weren't sure it was a real emergency, it was so quiet, but evacuated down & outside nonetheless.

Very few residents had come out, but we were advised to wait there.

After a while, a group of friends of my folks came by with my mother. They had taken her to have stitches sewn into a place on her cheek. My dad nor I had thought this wound was bad.

I saw, as if through a microscope, how the tissue of her thin, filmy skin had 3 clear sutures. There was no bandage on it. The layers had been sutured plumb together, & the knots' ends stood out from the skin like fancy white bows extending at least a quarter to a half-inch. What was unspoken was that Dad and I had been negligent, derelict.

The son of one in the group stopped by. He was a performer now & was off to record or to do a show.

I was out for a walk, & several adults tended an important fire in an indoor area. It seemed to be a bonfire, but was well contained, without a fireplace.

It was a vigil or was for teaching. Perhaps it was for smelting or smithery. I didn't know, but did not like it. I quickly poured water on to douse it & ran out & off.

Bean Kissing

I'd received a letter from a person at the secondary school I attended. "What do you go by?" It was from a man in administration, but not the Headmaster.

I showed it to people who were waiting to pick up students at the main entrance.

One was saying something about a boy I had dated. There was a photo projected onto an overhead screen of a curly-headed boy as a toddler, among others. She said, "Oh, that's Russel's grandson!" I wasn't sure who she meant by Russell.

A movie clip played them, these photos, for all of us to watch. It had been a school event, a party. There was a lot of food there, and Bernie got some dip on a haricot vert and said, "See if you like this." The bean was bright green, & his hair was very curly.

He put one end in his mouth, & held it in between his front teeth without biting down. I got the other end & bit it off. Of course our lips touched / kissed. He did it again & again. It was so funny to watch myself doing this, & I'd forgotten it had happened.

I then told how he & I had dated for 2 years.

The woman had to go to another entrance to pick up her student. An announcement alerted her. So she drove away. (It was Bernie's mum.)

Woman suffrage

The prof was lecturing fast & with gusto on the history of suffrage for women in the early 20th century. She said a word I didn't know, & I asked her to repeat it. She did. I asked again. She repeated. (I didn't know the word, but kept trying to write it down.) There were a few others of us in class.
I saw a photo of the woman in the discussion & said, "That's Emmeline! Emmeline Pankhurst!" I told how men had been attacked by governmental leaders that same day in another area of the same city. The men had been working on a street, repairing it. When it was investigated, it was found that these same men were attacked by the same attackers at the city hall & at the work site. We could see crude footage of the street venue, the men with their shovels.

A loud noise of shouting, jackhammering, and construction came from workers just outside our window, where a new wing of the building was going up. I looked out, & I think I must've shouted something. A young man looked right at me through the window across the short distance between us. It was as if we were 2 to 3 feet from one another.

The prof removed the wooden slat allowing the window to slam shut.

Another classmate mused, "I wonder how they knew" (the men were attacked in 2 places by the same men). I said I imagined they'd compared photos.

A squirrel slipped & caught itself as it scrambled down the huge tree trunk spanning up past our classroom. "Oh, that's right. It's open," I said, remembering.

The classroom had but 3 walls & a roof. The fourth wall was open. The professor was coming back in. So she had had to go downstairs to get outside and go over to tell the men to be quieter and now returned. We knew & admired how much she cared for us to have done it.

I looked down at the foot of the bed I sat in now. The others had gone. I was under the covers & there was a headboard at the foot of the bed (or I was in it backwards.) On a fabric tackboard of many primary colours were many photos of the boy who lived in this room. He was handsome & looked a bit like someone I knew, my brother perhaps.

I had a set of index cards laid out with reminders of what needed doing to complete my coursework in my classes.

I heard a child's laughter, shrill, & her footsteps, as she ran on the floor above. A man's voice talked to her. I supposed they were descending the staircase.

I looked over the head of my brother as he stood astride his bike & saw the most remarkable sight. Green leaves formed a lattice in the sky. They must have been clouds, but moved as if metallic parts being drug about by an invisible force & held aloft there. Perhaps a magnet drew them. I gesticulated & cried out, pointing up.

He looked, was of course astonished, & quickly tried to get a photo with his mobile, it was so unbelievable. By the time he snapped it, the image was already coming down, mutating, but may have been re-forming.

"Oh, it's a b'day party, I'll bet," I said. At the end of the cul-de-sac, the folks had rented a machine to fabricate this chicanery.

Library Job backtrack

I was at the bus stop, but didn't see the bus. A friend & fellow worker, Mari-lynda Seay, drove up. I thought she'd wait with me, but she said she often missed the bus, too. I got in & thought we'd go to a different stop to catch the bus, but she was driving all the way to work. She was a terrible driver!

At work, I didn't have a packed lunch nor £s
for one. I was going to ask a woman, Dell, for a
loan. But other women were shouting excitedly!
One had dropped her lunch, & it had cascaded down
a very icy slope & stopped. It was opened up &
looked like 2 large enchiladas, but intact. Further
down was a candy bar.

I agreed to try to recover it, if I could have
some of it. Everyone was scared. I looked around &
found a rope to secure around me & a small strong
tree growing on the terrace. I managed it / got it,
though the ramp was treacherously slick!

When I brought it back up to the fairly flat
upper area below the building access, a man with
whom I'd worked (Clay Daugherty) was on the
landing, & he had a French press. He was making &
drinking coffee. I didn't know he liked coffee.

I asked a woman teacher in the room by the
library if she liked the way the structural layout was
now. It had been 2 areas in 1, but each was now
closed off unto itself. She said it was all right, but
seemed hesitant. I went in.

I had a middle grade class in my library. The
room had silver, crystal-chandelier-like drapes on a
skylight, very high up in the vaulted ceiling. There
was a loud, booming AV programmed program that
was complex to operate & had so much info & bells
& whistles that it was impossible to manage or
glean much of anything from it. It did pose some
rhetorical questions. "What is existence?" There
were large, poster-sized cards that appeared on
holographic screens, & this, "What is existence?",
was on one. I put it to the students.

There were 2 boys sitting on a low bench
together. They dressed similarly, with long shorts &
tennis shoes with high socks. They looked very
young for their grade. One said, "This is my
boyfriend," though it was (already) apparent, as
they were inseparable, with the arm of one around
the other. The other child said, "My mum said not
to say that, yeh…" The word implied was 'yet', but
he didn't say it … yet, either.

Towering Superstructure of garbage

I was working, & on a previous day someone had
delivered many supplies (books?) to a remote
storage shed. Now a person at the store wanted 1 of
them, a book. It would be very difficult to locate, &
it was not a distinctive book nor in good condition.

To get there, I drove around the mall on the side
where the tower was. Located in the car park, this
tower was an extremely tall stack of garbage. The
base may have been in a dumpster, but it arose to an
improbable height, dozens of stories high. Each
square was distinct, & they were all merely stacked
one atop the other. You could make out where parts
of it were loosening and flaying in the wind like
huge, wide, thick sheets of orange, jelly-like
spaghetti. It could topple at any time. It was a major
draw.

I came back to work with 2 other women with me.
We had a box with some food. Each had to select a
lunchtime. I got the last. I ate a small bite of

something bland & dry. One of the women was welcomed by others into a work area apart from mine. They'd seemed welcoming enough & rather convivial as they told her of what was to be done.

Near the entrance of one of the stores (possibly ours) was a dinosaur model that would "go off", bellowing, & drips of water would fall down & shake off of it as it vibrated. I said to myself I would not like to work near it, as being so very unsettled so frequently would get old.

A man had an appt. with us. We told him we had no intention of buying his product. He didn't seem to mind, but had to be at the next appt. immediately, so asked the way. It was past the aeroport. I mentioned the name of the area, & names of streets & landmarks, but to my dismay, he seemed not to know our city at all. He left.

Week 3 - Sleepover

I was spending the night at a friend's house. We
each had a bed, & he had left the light on in the
walk-in wardrobe with both the wardrobe doors
open, so it was very bright. I got up & closed the
light.

I went upstairs to the attic where I had been many
months ago. I found large, open cardboard boxes. In
one were slices of hard, stale bread that I'd sliced
but not eaten. It had big craters in it from air
bubbles & a very crunchy crust. In another box was
bread that was bad. It had moulded & was filled
with rotten greyish-green filling.

Back downstairs, I saw a slideshow, a progression
of photos of my friend. Though he was white
before, he was now black. He was adorable in the
younger ones. Some were out of order, & in some
his father was depicted, again done as in a headshot
or occasionally with his son.

As a baby, a game was played where the toddler
was tossed into the air & caught in a <u>large</u> kettle.
Everyone would love & chant his name. He smiled.
They would put the lid on the pot. His name was a
type of code that needed deciphering.

Imprudent headmistress

At work, it was the 1st day back. Teachers were spread out in 2 huge adjacent auditoriums, one without tables. Many people had been preparing decorations for their classrooms & putting on silly costumes. A female had her pants turned under & had placed a dozen safety pins in straight horizontal lines on the outside of each pant leg below the knee. It was funny. The headmistress saw it & said, "Oh, you've got some pins showing." She thought it was by mistake. We all almost died, trying not to laugh.

The headmistress started going over important info & referred us to certain pages in our large workbooks that we needed to complete. I wandered into the next room, & nobody there could even hear her. So they didn't know, and wouldn't, what to do. Some teachers had gone as far as their rooms in other parts of the building.

———

Vicious, Old boss

I was at a jobsite where I had worked. My replacement was getting a feel for the job. She'd performed an analysis through a microscope. A former fellow colleague, Kat Partridge, asked how much I thought she should've charged. "£800?" she queried. "Oh, at least," I'd said in answer. She smiled, because I was right.

There would be a big show, & my former colleagues were helping me with a costume so I could sing with them. A woman, Juanita, who'd not been on the best of terms with me helped me with my costume. I was so pleased at this gesture. The gowns were of filmy yellow gauze that we split all the way down the middle. They went on over our clothing, reaching to the floor, and the effect was stunning.

The atmosphere was that of a country club. During rehearsal, I sang out loudly & very well, though I had just joined the group.

That night, we had (or may have) sung 1 number. But the whole excitement was surrounding this upcoming performance with the costumes. I was pulled from the show by my former boss. She also made it clear that I couldn't eat dinner there. It was because I had quit my job. The decision that I would not go on stage was irrevocable.

I drove many hours to get home, crestfallen, angry, & shocked at this reprisal.

The next day I was back. I'd left something in my former boss's office. I went in, & the item was there, as were a male Asst. & a man who worked for the production company. They'd be resetting for tonight's show.

The former boss came in & didn't say anything, but she seemed a <u>bit</u> contrite. She was cordial enough in person. She left a program from the night before on her desk & went out.

The production company worker was trying to maneuver around her desk. He drove a vehicle very quick, & very narrowly missed the desk! It may have been a front-end loader. The other man & I were floored, & the driver came back out from behind grinning. The Asst. who'd seen it happen said, "He's a fast driver!" We all laughed.

This Asst. had ties to the Community Outreach Group, & he got me to sign off on paperwork since I'd been there the night before. I must agree not to travel abroad for a designated time.

I saw 3 women, new employees, who I didn't know & a woman who'd worked with me for 20 yrs, but I didn't know well. We talked, sitting in a booth in a cafe' area. They were all very nice. I said I'd seen on the front of the programme about the pregnancies (of 3 women) and couldn't wait to know who was preggers. My former boss's voice came over the loudspeaker saying, "You can't know that unless you work here." I quietly said I just hoped to know who the women were who were preggers to the women seated there. They were all giving such apologetic looks. They wanted to tell me, but their hands were tied. My former co-worker, a black woman, had gone.

I walked out with one of the women, another black female. She said, "I heard you & liked your strong vibrato on the song last night." I said I had been ready to come on again, but had been pulled. She said, "Oh, girl, you were spinning like a top!" in regard to how angry I'd been.

There was a kid there getting things out of a storage area he'd just come out of. I was leaving, but asked him where his folks were. He was there alone. He said he had to do some work for school. I could tell he was lying & was living there. I alerted the Asst. about him before leaving.

Red Cherry, Blue Line

I had a new job. I was teaching young children a little about theatre. It was not clear-cut, so I had much leeway. I'd drawn a diagram on a large rectangular chapbook. I'd made the diagram of a stage & labelled it.

Some labels were presumably for labeling props & decor, such as a red cherry & a blue line. A boy got the diagram & sat in an easy chair with it. There were only a couple of kids, & it was casual seating. He really loved studying the chart.

There were large pieces of durable material, perhaps plastic, that lined up in a row. We lacked one to complete the set, but it had to be a specific type to fit.They had to interlock like a puzzle. We had at least 3 or 4. Once placed on a shelf, they appeared similar to books, with spines facing out.
We needed a gold one that was very hard & hard to find.

At long last, one was located and put on order. We got it in. In order to force it into place, it had to extend out of the shelf in the front, as it was larger than the rest. It clicked together, finally.

The kids were gone. An older woman who'd worked there a long time said, "Oh, look at this one. Here's 'Red Cherry, Blue Line'." When we looked at the new one, it was white, squishy, & round, puffed out on all sides like a big marshmallow sandwich cake, but the size of an overgrown portobello mushroom.

I came in one day, & a sweet young woman was there, as were our male boss & other men. I could hear our boss talking excitedly on the phone in his tiny office with its door open, probably to a relative. He was a kind man.

There was an area on the wall that formed a built-in rack to place our keys upon arrival. The rack had slots on it, & I hung my key on the second from the left. Some of the circles had colourful scenes on them. Mine was empty. As soon as I put my keys on the rack, the boss, whose office was but a few feet away, stopped talking mid-sentence because I'd cut him off.

He came out & patiently showed me where to hang my keys (& where NOT to hang them.)

All Plastic

"All plasticky, that way." A young woman didn't like her new coat very well. It had a hood. I had a new one like it, too. They were plasticized. We were in a grocer's, at a sitting area. I showed her how to loosen the jacket too, for casting it off.

An old man went to the chemist counter. His script wasn't there. He left, very dejected. They went abruptly after him in the car park to track him down presumably to give him some information. I hoped they had found his meds.

I took off to go through the aisles. I walked around an end cap that had a clipboard on top with papers. The clipboard was attached to a shrink-wrapped package for me, having been left there atop the display. The employees knew I would somehow see it & pick it up at one point. It was a few books.

The grocer's departments were very small but had a lot of customers. We were getting breakfast. I was going to be leaving.

The mother of the family wanted more bread (sweetish bread). We went to that department. They had very little: one package the woman would even want, yellow/orange. It was very dear! She couldn't get it; was shocked at the price! I had a new car and didn't know the area but said I could go get something (in the morning - implied). There were so few places. She was hesitant. I had said I'd "get doughnuts." Then I said I'd get "bagels." She brightened and said - "Okay, if there were bagels." She tried telling me where it was that I'd need to go, but I didn't know the way very well at all.

Wizardry

Globe of water had a little, brown, twig-like shoot that was living. It looked like lightning. The water swirled. The twig hung down, suspended from nothing, from the top.

It was not a true globe. Very few, if any, had got this to work; to live, & then to <u>stay</u> alive!

The wizard watched me to see if I could do it. I would have to invert it, keeping the twig intact.

Suspense. The world needed this to happen.

Perilous driving w/ young son

There was a computer game where you could light up letters on the screen to spell out the word to answer the question. I had a young son.

On t.v., I thought the commentator said there were educators on a trip to the Continent. The feed showed arms & bodies of people I recognized however, & I doubted they were all on the Continent. You could hear their voices, & I worked with them at a school in the UK. The talk was excited sounding, for there had been a water leak. Maybe the sprinkler system had malfunctioned.

I had to get to work. I took my son in the car. It was very dark out, & the road was vast. A couple of drivers with no headlights on drove awful fast right at our car, one right after another, narrowly missing us! A car had flipped in the middle of the road. I wasn't sure, due to looking at the road, but there may have been a couple of bodies hanging upside down from the top of the car, now on its side. I said, "Look, but only if you want to."

A half block away, it was full daylight. A squadron of military personnel were in the road, perhaps 50 or so men in full uniform, standing at attention. I saw I could not drive by, for the road was barricaded by a huge, russet orange wall of rusted piled up vehicles. These completely blocked even a glimpse of the view where I needed to drive.

I stopped my car, got out, & asked. One man said, "You can't go there. That is not a road." I frowned deeply! It was Glendale, and I knew it. Another man standing there said, "It is a road. It's blocked, so you'll have to go another way." He seemed very uncomfortable at the first man's lie & apologetic.

I drove back the way we'd come, but it was not easy, since I had always taken the route that was now closed. At a store, I pulled into the car park to

get my bearings. A woman teacher who I knew,
Jolinda, was on the front corner step under the
store's awning looking at me. She said, "I have you
in 5 minutes." This meant she would be back at
work & would drop her class at my library by then.
I said my son had been sick.

At work, the water leak was no longer a
problem. One little girl was in the library, in need of
1 specific, large, non-fic. book. The place was
deserted except for us & dimly lit. I found the book!
She looked genuinely grateful, but didn't smile or
say anything as she clutched it to her breast.

An assistant came & said, "Here are the 2
times in the schedule that I was telling you about,
when there is no one here." She meant that kids had
been there returning books before we were slated to
report back. She showed a long horizontal list of
times with the 2 problem areas denoted.

Swimming near World-Famous Cave

My cousin and I were swimming in the sea. We
were at a small cave-like opening above which hung
a sign telling its name. The wall of golden-brown
limestone in which it was set was huge, extending
up and out in all directions, as far as the eye could
see. The water was vividly blue and deep.

She and I were in a fine mood, the day was so
perfect. I had a huge atlas that I opened as we
treaded water. I consulted the 1st page I opened it

to. It showed the very place where we were. It was totes famous, but of course only a dot on the map.

I was very excited that this had happened, as it boded well for us. We went in.

The artifacts inside were very dated, but somewhat modern. Everything was dry & dusty.

There was an oven that was labelled. A male voice that I'm pretty sure was my deceased father's voice told what to do. The oven had to have a certain metal lip removed from one area to be operable.

Another woman was in the cave with us now, my aunt. A very small boy, possibly a cousin, joined us, too. There was a typed list of foods one could make. We were going to make something, & it would probably be biscuits.

Restaurant Woes

I was in a nice restaurant. A young woman with long, blonde, loose, beautiful hair said she was covering another girl's shift. She told her fellow male server & me that this colleague hadn't even bothered to double check to see if she was really picking up the shift for her.

At the daily lineup, the woman filling in had her back to the front door. She was rapt, as they all were, in the goings on. I saw another young woman

with sparkly, wavy, platinum hair bounce in,
approach the group, note the blonde girl, turn & left.

Afterwards, I asked the first woman if the
one she was subbing for had silver hair, & she
brightened and said, "Yes!" She was glad to know
her mate had bothered to check in on the situation.

I ate with her & a couple of males in a quiet,
dark room where employees could eat when not in
use. The conversation was quiet & rather dark.

When I came out, dozens & dozens of
people from another land were in the restaurant.
They were there to eat, but their customs were very
different from ours. The women were eating in a
large room, but the men had come out. They lined
the hallways, always standing still, facing the same
way, single file. They would smoke thin cigarettes;
even the teens. Maybe this was why they weren't in
the dining area. They wrapped round the
restaurant's public swimming pool with its glass
windows, or mere open air in some spots. Some
banged drums quietly. It took a long time to get the
food ordered & served.

I left afoot, circling round the block & was
going back toward where my whole family was
staying on holiday. But on my way, adjacent to the
restaurant one street over, my husband & 1 young
son came cutting through the gardens of some
houses excitedly from the direction I'd come. They
said, "Come on!" They turned about, and I

followed. We would've now been heading back in the direction of the restaurant.

The restaurant also had a small indoor pool beside its front door for employees only, & it was visible as we entered the front. I think there was a female swimming at the time. We went right by it and through, into a hall where we queued up with many relatives to place our orders.

There were many items on tall worktops along the hall we passed through. Most were foods. Some were cakes. One large, fancy sandwich cake had 'Take Me' spelled out in colourful decorative frosting on its top. All these foods, we decided, were free for people who were too needy to buy things. I saw an empty package & realised I had taken & eaten the food out of it myself.

We finally ordered & paid, though it was a long ordeal. When the food was brought, Janis's wasn't brought out, & they had no record of its being ordered. She is my brother's wife. Our mother was to have ordered with a BOGO-½-off deal. Mum said then that she guessed she had done it. But we checked the receipt, & she had not. It was sad.

We played a little music on the way back to the hotel and I sang, at the suggestion of some.

Night of Danger

I had to go get my belongings back. It was very late
at night in a dangerous, rural area. A woman with
me knew I was going and worried, as did I, but it
had to be done.

It took a long time to get there & wasn't easy to
find, but I found it. I was so glad that I went in &
told some girls the tale. They were allowed to get
up and hear it. It was more exciting than a film, as
they listened in their pyjamas. They got into the
paper sack where they slept so they'd grow ripe. I
barely squeezed in, and I sang my epic tale to them.

I'd found my things, but hadn't recovered them. A
patrol officer saw them, including the gun & the
ammo strewn beside it.

The mother of the girls was the woman who'd been
so concerned about me all along. It was she who let
this female patrol officer know I'd be coming.

Spidery Masks and a Front-end Loader

I am going to eat with many relatives at a
restaurant. It is around Halloween. My cousin's
father whom she hadn't seen in 30 yrs. is purported
to be there. It's a nice fast-food place.

People are driving with costumes on. Several wear
full red & blue Spiderman masks. One, evidently
handknit, is unravelling so that it looks like red &

blue webbing through which the driver is being forced to try to see through.

A man is attempting to pull a huge, orange pipe on a front-end loader into a very tight spot. He's wearing a mask so he can't see well. Another chap is sitting on the right edge of the platform, next to the pipe, in a type of sidecar.

The driver zips in front of us, cutting us off. He misses a large obstruction, like a brown wall or huge brown piece of furniture by millimetres. The man crouched on the little ledge has a panic-stricken look on his face, but is unscathed. He jumps off & runs off.

I'm at a professor's house, but she's not there. I curl my hair. It is as if I tried to make a finger curl, but I haven't done it lately, & if it works it will be a slender pipe going straight up on the top of my head. I smile at this crazy image.

I curl all my hair in one more large curl. I see my reflection in a large mirror. I'm wearing a stunning black dress, & the curl is great! I really need some hairspray. I look under her bathroom counter. There's stuff everywhere, but no luck.

Walking through a sitting room with hardwood floors, I see a lot of white stuff drying that's been spilled or sprayed on the floor. I quickly scoop up a handful hoping for hairspray. Alas, it's shave cream! I can tell immediately by its smell & taste.

Oh, yes, I remember now that she's married. Her husband must've accidentally done this.

No Tent Pole nor Telescopic Fishing Pole

We were at a community centre. I helped out there, clearing brush off the court before games, etc. The schedule for when we were to report was erratic. I asked the young woman in charge what time we would get started tomorrow. She was distracted, watching a basketball game in play. She said she didn't know for sure. I reworded the question, & she said to call the office.

My older son was playing. He was doing pretty well, but he was wearing loose strap-like rubber sliders over his socks. One was much too loose, or maybe it was a medical boot.

A few minutes later, my younger son was playing. We called him over at a timeout. A woman gave him a shot in his upper arm. He really winced & mouthed, "Ow!" He hadn't seen that coming. We hadn't told him.

I went to the now empty hostel and walked up several flights to my room. I went in & crossed the bedroom to the loo. I really needed to go. I flushed the toilet afterward & washed my hands. I made my way out of the loo and froze.

I saw a long, slender pole with a white gauze stuck on the end extending from a white sheet that was wrapped around, tent-like, between the twin bed and the wall.

I looked into the space. A big man was hunkering in there with malevolent looks. "You can go. I won't tell on you," I said. The pole-gun remained trained on me! "Don't kill me! I'm just a girl!" I screamed as I burst out through the door, through the hall, into the stairwell, & down the stairs. I had to get down to the main desk to tell them what was going on.

Purple and Blue Sheet and a Near Miss

My husband was about to drive our oldest son back to his home, so I told the middle son to hurry or he'd be left behind. They'd leave to get something to eat & come right back for him. We had to go through a lot of stuff to decide what he'd take, clothes & toys, etc. A good deal of it had to be washed out in the front garden by hand. Also, we, together with the youngest son, were frantically putting finishing touches on our art work.

I saw that my neighbour was in her front garden across the street, taking in her wash. She had a pretty, deep purple & royal blue print sheet. The same pattern was on our favourite comforter that was drying in our garage. I went in through our open garage door & pulled ours off of the car where it was lying to flat dry. I hollered across at her, "We love that pattern, too," as I held it up for her to see.

"It goes with everything," she said gaily.

"It's also the favourite of the teacher who taught across the hall from me." I confided. I thought about the coincidence that both these women were black. As I gazed at this coverlet, I noticed for the 1st time an inset. It was an image of a large gold frame surrounding 3 cute girls lying on their stomachs & smiling out, with their chins propped on their hands.

The car I'd gotten the blanket off of wasn't in gear. The garage door on that side of the garage was open now, & this car, my husband's pride & joy, was starting to drift slowly down the driveway, picking up speed. I was so worried as I tried to stop it with my hands as I walked beside it. I managed to slow it and alter its direction as it headed toward the road. Now it was heading almost directly at my son's car that was parked on the side of the road at the foot of the drive!

I brought it to a stop, with great relief. The coverlet was on the car again. Getting in & reaching through the open window, I yanked the sheet up. "Oh!" I cried when I saw the other car's wing right there! This car was touching the other car, but had stopped at exactly the right millisecond. Neither had incurred damage!

Wild Child and dull pre-party

I was at work in my big, private, airy ofc. A man
from the Central Ofc. had asked me to sign off on
paperwork that I'd returned, but I'd forgotten to
stop in and do it … again. A woman came into my
ofc. - showed me where to sign. It had to be done on
a certain tiny blank. It might have been an NI
Number, too. I had a little trouble with it. I felt
badly that she'd had to drive over just for that. She
said the man had wanted me to get the credit due
me.

We walked around the building a bit. The new
policy was to not air condition it & to leave outside
doors standing open. Some hammered metallic
archways near an exterior door had rusted, but
overall it was a pleasant change from being too
cold. After going upstairs & back, the visitor had
left, so I went back to my ofc.

There were loud voices coming from a little blond-
headed girl who sat in her blue dress in a student
desk in the middle of a wide well-lit hallway. She
screamed pejoratives & was wildly upset, visibly!
Her younger sister was in another student desk
behind her, facing the same way, but was calm.

The Headmistress & Assistant Headmaster were
talking about what shocking act this older girl had
perpetrated the night before. She was a devil.

There would be a drinks party that evening in someone from the office's home. I didn't plan to go, but many would attend. Several women stayed after hours and were having after-work drinks with our headmistress in preparation for the party. Every one of them sat spaced far apart around a large table.

Though they were drinking, they seemed not to be enjoying it, as if it were a requisite activity. They would take a drink, sigh, talk a little in a desultory, downhearted way, & mostly stare at one another, at their drinks, or into space.

Some drinks were wines, one was a dark brownish-purplish substance that did not appear frothy. Maybe it was a mixed drink, but I didn't see or hear ice clinking in it.

Later, a man came excitedly in to consult the administrators. I believe the other women had gone. The headmistress showed me his idea that he explained like this. He could design & build a contraption that would fit to the wild girl's buttocks so well, precisely, & tightly, that she could not get up, but it wouldn't harm her in any way. They were thrilled. Since I was about the size of their young pupil, they wanted to let him try it out on me.

I wasn't so sure about that!

Dog (and Pony?) Show at Church

I visited my home church after many years of nonattendance. They'd hosted a neighbourhood dog show there that day. One dog in particular was an especially fine specimen in size alone, if nothing else. It was a very dark Great Dane. I would say it was black. Its owner looked like she was so proud & in love with this beast.

Now the dinner was almost ready. There were 2 large pots. One of the dishes called for many ingredients that were unavailable, so it would be served plain. You could see many bits dropping like beads of necklaces into 1 pot from above, but none going into the other. Folks gathered as a woman played a piano that was right beside the stove. Though I'd not been there in decades, I remembered the words of all the verses of the next song she played, a hymn. There was only one hymnal & a man seated near the piano bench was looking on at it, as he sang while she played. They'd changed the words on some of the later parts, inclusive language and all. Consequently, I messed up the lyrics on some of it.

There was a printed programme of sorts that mostly had churchwide news in it. I read it and saw that 1 item would be worth giving a mention, so I raised my hand during announcements & pointed out that next Mon. would be the art class & they still needed materials donated.

One man said I should start teaching Italian classes, too. I agreed to sign up to teach 1 Italian class. Another said they needed helpers for the art class still, so I should come help that night, too. I said I would. This continued for some time. I had wanted to say how lovely-ly the pianist had played while we were arriving, but didn't have a chance.

The big dog's owner (or shall I say significant other?) came bustling in saying abruptly and concernedly some of his, the dog's, things had been left behind at the dog show; & what's more, he was missing!

We all commenced searching. Some looked in small spaces, such as little cupboards. I said, "He can't be in there! He's the size of a horse, practically!"

The owner said, "He's not that big."

"Well, he's as big as a pony. He's a pony!" I declared. We all looked & looked, to no avail.

Sweet, Sick mum

I was back from a film shoot, & my good friend, Mitch Mitchie, always wanted me to check in after my aeroplane touched down. He supplies me with a white backpack with a walkie talkie in it.

I walked across from the airport to the beach & got a little free refreshment that was set up at an

openair stand. This late, nobody was awake. I called
Mitch. Good friends are gems.

The next time I travelled, I had the pleasure
of again working with 3 acquaintances. Though we
weren't in the same scenes, we took the same flight
home.

One was a man about my age. Another was
a woman who'd been a year ahead of me in school.
She was easily recognizable by her poise, hourglass
figure that she'd kept, & engaging voice. The third
was a much younger closed-mouth lad.

We older ones were walking together in the
aeroport when we saw the young alumnus demurely
give me a nod as he stepped into a revolving door.
His wavy hair & good looks were easy to spot.
"He's worked on shows with us before, hasn't he?"
one asked. "Oh, yes," I replied.

The other man was the next to part company
with me. While you waited for your baggage, you
were seated in a waiting area & aeroport personnel
matched your belongings to you. He got his shoes.
Since those were all he was still waiting on, he left.

I had so much to carry. I looked in a large,
deep bag, & saw that I'd not taken out my big,
white backpack from the last trip yet; but here was a
smaller white one, so predictable & responsible was
my friend.

I now had my shoes & other things, but I was still waiting on one last item. I asked an employee, since I hadn't been paiged. The person said, "Look." It was right there. They were very efficient & yet, they hadn't called. I remembered that they were wont to do this, just let us find our things unlike the others.

As I collected them, I saw that my fellow alumna's mother had come to retrieve her. The mum asked what I thought about her daughter's situation. I said she seemed to be doing fine. Her mum said, "Have you looked at her closely?" I did then. Rather than seeing her silhouette and glimpsing the profile as we walked abreast, I looked full on at her face.

Her features were disfigured. Her huge eyes protruded grotesquely, and the lenses were clouded. The scleras were bulging, opaque. "Can she see?" I asked. Her mum said she could, but not well, due to the disease. They were readying to leave. The woman's daughter had her baby at home to tend to.

"I love babies!" I said. She, the baby's mum, brightened.

"Well, make sure you come by to visit, or have one of your own, better yet." she said, in a cheerful way.

"So it's not too soon for 'the ask' on a first date?" I asked.

She laughed heartily & said, "No, it's not!"

It was a little hard to check in with my
friend with so much stuff, but I managed it.

Week 4 - Mission

We had to get back to the building to recover our equipment from the raid. I was driving a British van, but in the right lane, for we were not in the UK. I was 16. I had my husband, his brother, & others with me. The speed limit was 70 km/h & I was going 70, but it seemed we were flying, the other cars straggled so. I passed them recklessly on the right. The speed limit would soon change to 90. Time was of the essence.

Then there were dozens of cars stopped in the two right lanes, lining the road. Computer & cell phone screens and news cameras were all trained on the building to our left.

One colour shot, an image of what they were all photographing, showed mostly a red & blue image framed in black. The photo was summarily blown up (enlarged) & made into a large, car-sized box. The other five sides were solid black. It was a secure box in which people could cast votes. This prototype was emulated but a few times, but its idea was used to make very many bright, neon green pods. These were much smaller, made of shiny, shellacked metal, like open flower blossoms with wide gaping petals. When folded in (down), they made secure voting pods.

I drove along, albeit slowly, in front of (to the left of) these vehicles, in between them & the object of their acute interest. Oh, yes, it was right next to where we were going, so the hubbub was understandable!

The queue of people thronging the building we also needed to gain entry to was at a standstill. Nevertheless, we bypassed them by walking right past them, in, & through the packed lobby. A security official saw us, of course, & waved us thru when he saw who we were.

We had to get everything we'd left, & it was interspersed around. We split up, each going to different wings. All the articles would be gathered in one huge storage room in the back of the building. It took quite awhile, even though we rushed.

Outside this back room, a carnival atmosphere pervaded. Children were unattended. I saw the girl we required right away. A gorgeous, young thing, dressed well, in matching leopard print shorts & top & sandals, she was 5 or so years old. Rather than tip my hand, I gave the prompt that she knew so well to another precious girl standing beside her.

The original girl we needed to work with pouted and took the bait, saying, "That's what you ask me!" We got her to come easily then. She got in the van, but I had to go in to retrieve the rest of the gear.

I got it out onto the high roof & was perched on the tall extension ladder, but I got off balance. The ladder teetered & fell. I was hanging from the ledge! One of the young assistants was on the roof with me. He ran over & pulled me up a bit, first by one hand only and then with both hands. I helped by hoisting my legs up & onto the roof. It had been a close call!

Some taller men dangled & then dropped, but the ladder was soon replaced. I took the van back. Everyone was gone but this child & this same close associate, also 16 like me. We had to scare the girl straight to get her to go back home. I opened and coaxed her with pantomime to reach in and touch my maw with her forefinger. I closed my eyes.

When I opened them a moment later, she was far off down the road. My friend pointed her out to me, as he'd been watching the whole time. Her unmistakable, cute figure was disappearing into an open culvert beside the road. We redistributed the heavy equipment. It had gone all right.

torturous Algorithm of death

Books were sorted onto shelves in the collection manually. Also, a computer generated program went about sorting books by the colour of book spines.

Once the colour hit the shades of red, mulberry, or any point after that in the algorithm colour spectrum, this called for a human death.

This is what the young man who lived in the home/library was waiting for. Once it clicked over, & there was 1 computer generated loss of life, he could kill undetected. He was methodical. While there was no way he'd kill prior to the sanctioned time, he laid the groundwork.

The torture went on for some time. There was a female kept in captivity, but she was not the target. She was a foil to draw attention away.

It ticked over.

The boy's death at the hand of the masterful one did not happen immediately, so engrossed was he in the elaborate & long suffering torment. But it didn't take too long.

The workers all took part in destroying evidence in between continuing to shelve books by sorting them. The library was now open to a few, though it was still not entirely done.

Evidence was placed in black tubs. It would all be destroyed later. Mostly, it was hair & body parts, & of that like.

An old man was searching for a particular title (B Fis). It showed that it was in/available on the OPAC, but it was not locatable.

One young man working with a few others overheard & said, "Oh, that one's here," handing the book over to us to be checked out.

The patron was disapproving as, frankly, was I. This was not as it should've been, not where it'd belonged. I asked & was told matter-of-factly that they were putting dozens of titles in this hodgepodge section with no rhyme nor reason. Evidently it was easier. I and the elderly gentleman were baffled to the point of almost being unbelieving. This was idiocy & laziness at its finest.

my Seminar

There was a huge family event going on in a large room with columns, a school cafeteria. On the pillars were posters that helped one learn to recognize letters, aid learning to read, and offer pneumatic devices. There would be a very large capital letter, more wording, and bright, colourful designs to accompany the written words. I saw this on one: **B**egin with these for health - B, C, D, E (vitamins). There was also a beautiful butterfly.

I went down the hall a ways and entered a more enormous room where I would preside over an all-day seminar. Dozens of people were already assembled. I noticed that many children were there with their parents. I went through this area to the next gigantic space adjacent to it. This one had levelled seating and looked to have the capacity to easily hold 300 or more. There was a smattering of people in there. I saw the woman who'd signed me up just yesterday to teach this course on how to engage and teach children. Her bright blue hair, cut in a short wave, was pretty. It stood out. She was with her husband. They were excited to see me, as they'd be if they'd seen a celebrity, unlike the ones who'd signed up to attend today and sat staring straight ahead, zombie-like. She said she could stay for a few minutes, but would be leaving.

I noticed the tall projection screens had the name of the seminar, time, room numbers, etc., projected on them. I had been meaning to write my contact info on these white boards, but now it would be impossible. I would have to walk around and type the info in later, so it could project up on the screens while the people waited. Shoot! Another dead air time. I knew most presenters would have developed a plan, an agenda, and more than likely many power points. I was going to wing it, however.

The woman drew my attention to little cubicles that lined one area. They looked like individual, stand-alone sidecars or little rides at a fair one would get in on a track to go spinning around in. These were royal blue. I got in one. They were organs or could be played as a piano when seated inside. The sound could be heard from both rooms. I told her I wouldn't use it. She said, "Well, you could always sing." I decided it would be nice to sing "You are the Wind Beneath My Sails" as a sendoff after I'd succeeded in leading my whole-day seminar.

She also showed me a place I could take them that had an outdoor seating area, a bit like a Greek amphitheatre. I asked if they were supposed to bring children to this seminar, and she said, "No, of course not." I didn't know how to tell the ones who had done so that they shouldn't have, now that they'd done it. I verified with her how long to afford them for a lunch break. I wondered if she would leave her contact info for me. Then she was gone.

It was at least 15 minutes after the time this was to have begun. I didn't think I could stall any longer. "Okay," I said, shouting out to them, "we're going to get started. You can move to be nearer one another, so you won't have to be in two areas, if you like." Nobody moved. "We're going to start by standing and taking a break because I see that many have already been sitting still with nothing to do for awhile. So you can walk in place or jog in place for a couple of hours. Oh, I mean a couple of minutes." I laughed nervously. It had been a Freudian slip.

I would tell of the benefits of reading aloud, but decided to start with something more exciting. There were some cosplay costumes. I had everyone move to the outdoor area. The costumes were lined up. I said I would need volunteers. Then I picked the volunteers from amongst the children in the audience. There were 10 costumes, gorillas, snakes, cowboys, etc. I looked at the plasticized bi-fold description leaflets for each costume then and saw that each character also needed a person to present it. So there would have to be time allotted to allow them to read over it and prepare to present their sidekick character, I decided with an inward groan.

The blue-haired enlistment woman was seen in the distance in an unloading area, putting crates of materials out the back door of her former art classroom. She was quitting her job as a teacher here. She had a woman helping her.

I announced that I would need 10 volunteers, and I saw one blond girl who I'd earlier noticed reading one of the plaques aloud in the cafeteria, so I knew she was able to read though she was around 5 or 6. I called her up and told her in a stage whisper that she would be like the snake's handler if she'd accept this role. She was down with it.

This day was shaping up to be a doozy.

Government job - FREE food

Everyone needed to perform a number of activities, but the ones they were to complete were not all the same. Some could buy certain foods. Many actions had to do with collecting receipts with certain codes, but these were quite involved. Or you could try to hit a large object with a spongy ball remotely. It had to be timed by a governmental employee. The spacing had to be measured precisely, and it had to hit within 3 tries while on the phone with the public agent.

I discussed this with many of my older female relatives. I was surprised to have found that quite a few opted for the collecting of the codes alternatives. It seemed rather tedious to me, as well as mysterious, since I'd never checked into all the ins and outs of how to do those.

At a restaurant, multiple coupons were handed out for free dishes. Ideally, you would come eat there to get these free meals, but it didn't exactly state that. So I got many of them while I was there. The problem with using the coupons was that the products stipulated were often unavailable. For this reason, I saw nothing wrong with getting available macaroni and cheese trays while I could. Never mind the fact that the restaurant had just now closed, and the workers had left. I was sure they didn't mind. I got quite a few and told other patrons about them, too. One was a former co-worker who looked a bit askance at my alerting her to the fact that the food was there for the taking. I paid her little to no heed.

Later, a woman called me at home to try to hit the object with the small, airy ball. I was pretty upset that my husband had disassembled the setup. Now the distance would have to be measured again, and the place I was to stand would need remarking, all while she waited on the line. She sounded old as dirt. My husband helped me, as well he should have, when he saw my dismay.

Though she would say when to toss the ball and I would do so at her command, it would float over and flutter down, and miss. Every time! She would have to complete an additional task. This one was not going to be counted.

At holiday time, there was such a problem with people placing big, recyclable plastic containers in rubbish bins at work. I got some out and others helped me, seeing how bad the problem was. The insensitivity people had for the earth was shocking, not to mention their ignorance, if they weren't doing this out of mere laziness or callousness.

The unParty and Look Out!

At work, it was the last day for one assistant, and another one working there would be taking over. It was as if it were the replacement's first day because I was telling her what to do, but she seemed not to know what I meant. I began showing her how to do the seemingly simple task of putting books that were out of order back in order on shelves. But I found I couldn't tell her how to do it well or easily because at least 9/10th of the books were out of order. Whole sections would need to be reconfigured, a more difficult and time consuming task to grasp and perform.

There were several gallons of milk sitting in a little red wagon.

Some people took sheets off the bed and put them into the refrigerator to solve the problems we were experiencing. I had seen this before, but I didn't think that seemed the best fix. One of the computers that was very large did appear to be stuck, as in nonfunctional. I saw on the screen that someone was trying to call in, or a message was waiting in the queue to go out, but nothing happened. Then the person I was needing to contact called in and got through to me, after all.

He worked at a supermarket in a town where I lived. I said I'd been trying to get in touch with him. He said I needed to repay the £43.00, but I said, "No, that is what you owe me. I have been waiting so long to get this!" This was met with dead air. I thought he might have been mad, or the line had been lost again. "I can come there after work. Will you be there then?" I asked.

"You must pay us £43.00." he replied.

"No, that's the amount you owe me," I repeated. "I can be there in a half an hour." The line went dead. I now realised I had a dozen things that I had to do immediately after work.

During this time, women had been coming into the room. A few were from other schools, I suspected. I knew one of them. Others were from other areas of our school. Scant nibbles were laid out on top of a computer here and a worktop there, along with a punch bowl with punch. The food comprised a

sandwich cake that looked obviously and somewhat
pitifully decorated in a very amateurish fashion, and
other unappealing fare. The people had been getting
a little of the food, and I'd say the atmosphere was
that of a wake, though I'd never attended one. Not
one person smiled or said anything.

I was so mad because it was clear this had been
planned behind my back. Whether it was to keep me
in the dark, make me look bad, like an uncaring
employer not even having deigned to participate in
planning and providing a going-away party for this
longtime employee, or both, I didn't know. I highly
suspected this high amount of low pettiness was for
both purposes.

After these visiting people had left, I again saw the
milk that had been sitting out, possibly for days. It
still was. I said, "Oh, I meant to refrigerate that."

"That was why I had it in the crate, to keep it cold,"
said the assistant who was on her way out, in every
sense of the word. I knew the two gallons on the
ends of the wagon had been chilled, so I tried to
make a note to check the middle two gallons so
we'd drink them first, if they'd not soured.

We'd all left the library when I realised I needed my
car key. It was in the now locked library, as was my
key to the library. Another fellow employee was
still in the building and was belligerently pleading
on her mobile that she needed help getting a
shipment. Her young sons were behind her in the

hallway, and she was near hysterical. "So you have someone here, … now? At the school? Okay, well good. He needs to bring it in by the gymnasium door." She hung up. It seemed as if this was a miracle! A young man who must have been a security guard for the school system came right in with a big shipment. She put one of the packages, a large object, on a huge cart and carted it off with one of her sons, presumably to her room.

I picked up another of them. It weighed about a pound and a half. It was a huge net with large air-filled balls at the bottom that looked like balloons. I supposed they were buoys, or the like. I told her other elementary-aged son to take this to her. He was big for his age, blond, with short, tight waves in his hair, and his face was flushed deep red, for he was crying so hard and couldn't stop. He had been crying when his mum was there, too, so I thought nothing of it.

When the child had gone, I told the guard how upset I was that my keys were locked in the library, and I couldn't get in. He quietly spat out, "I can let you in. I'm Breem." He didn't like his name, but felt he had to keep using it to see if he could overcome his dislike for it. I could tell by the way he was talking and looking at me that he knew me. He had undoubtedly been one of my students there, probably 18 or 19 years ago or so. I stared long and hard at his face but could see no resemblance nor recall any young version of this incertain man.

We got in all right. I was still flummoxed, so I now let him know that. This was because the key to my car was in a compartment in the huge computer that was now either still frozen or was frozen again. The small tray it was in wouldn't open if it wasn't on. He said, "Oh, I can get it on."

He lifted the small, square mouthpiece of plastic with its rounded corners and its upper and lower pieces fused together, out of which a thin wire hooked onto the large contraption, and he apparently tased this little piece with the instrument he'd used to blow the lock on the door.

Sparks shot out in all directions, and there was an ominous silence as we sensed or perhaps also saw the shockwave going up the wire into the machine. Then the entire contraption began shaking, beeping, lighting up, and smoking, and it was about to blow up. He and I looked at one another as if to say, "Oh, shit!"

Fattening us up, with New Hire/s?

I had been rehired at a former workplace. There was a new assistant who I'd not yet met. I went into the library where I would work, and a fellow teacher I'd worked with brought in a large box for me. It was opened, and we saw several tall, colourful bottles in the shape of a cartoon character. Each held topical germ killer. Another teacher came, saw these, and asked how to use them. They were so tall, I wondered if there could be trouble with young children. I said they might be pumped, but care would have to be taken not to splatter the eyes.

There was coffee in a huge, open area for teachers. The carafes were high up on ledges, and these worktops were spaced well apart. Beside each huge coffee container was a plate with a single piece of pie. It looked like cherry, with a layer of white, probably cream cheese or mascarpone and whipped cream. There were many teachers getting food and drink and milling about, but none of us had on masks. We did our best to maintain some distance.

A woman I'd not met was having trouble getting coffee, as it looked like it was nearing the end so it was almost empty, and she also wanted a dessert. Her hands were oversized, each finger puffier than a doughy cream puff. I thought she had elephantiasis of hands. She was cheery nonetheless. I sought to help her. She held the plate out and over to me. I got the coffee cup on there, alongside the pastry. She may have brushed my hand, or thought she'd done so, for she said brightly, "My hands are clean!"

A friend who I now worked with again said, "Look, there's fish fillets over here!" She was filling a bag with takeaway. She was standing in a separate aisle, also replete with multitudinous rich, sweet treats, all free. I wondered what was up and if the head teachers were trying to fatten us all up.

When I returned to the library, a woman I supposed was now my assistant was seated on the floor. She

had her knees drawn up under her sweater. I
assumed she may not be able to walk upright. She
was wonderful, with a pronounced accent. Her
accent and looks led me to believe that she was
from Asia, and probably Western Asia, at that. She
said that the name of the program we used here was
the same as the one they'd had where she'd worked
before.

I told her a short folktale with implications not easy
to grasp. She looked puzzled, so I could tell she
didn't get the meaning. I would explain through
pantomime and rewording. Another blunt woman
who spoke with a beautiful African accent cut me
off somewhat rudely. Maybe she'd said, "No
matter." So the moment had passed, and I no longer
tried to explain the meaning of the tale. This woman
speaking to me with the lovely African accent was
now my assistant.

She could stand now, and her skin was a pretty,
deep brown. She said the name of our workplace
was also the name of the workplace where she had
worked, and from where she was recruited to fill
this opening. I asked who'd interviewed her, and
she said, "Grandma," matter of factly. I didn't say a
word, but found this (reference to our headmistress)
to be at once concise, precise, clever, and irreverent.
I liked her very much!

I needed to ask the administration if I could not
have patrons today. I realised the kids could not
return books anyway since they had not checked out

any. I thus decided to suffice with my emailing the faculty to hold all comers without asking prior. I would take charge of this situation. This was my newly determined, proactive way.

There were children in the queue to check out books. They stood at the end where I was, the opposite end of the banque from where books would come in. There was what looked like a large cash register, but the children in line were too close to it and to one another. One was a tall, blond, unsmiling girl I'd known to be a troublemaker. I told her to go back to class, and took the books from her. She left. Another got too close. I told that child to go back. For some reason, I was now sitting on the floor. Perhaps one had shoved me, but if so, it was a small child. I wasn't hurt. The next student was older and tall and got too close, but then sidestepped the worktop, came behind, and made as if to touch me with one hand. "Go back to class!" I commanded. He left.

A couple of more well-behaved kids got books and went back to class.

I was trying to show the new woman how to shelve the books, but the system was complicated. To start with, low level books went by level and the author's first initial of last name. The section was very jumbled. I'd been gone so long, it was in woeful disrepair with almost no way to visualize a system.

Actors and Accidents

A production company had brought a crew to our house to build a set for a show. A big yellow steamroller was rolling up extremely quickly toward the front door. Whoever was driving did not detect how close it was to the house, and it burst the door down!

From inside the front parlor, we saw the door explode in, saw the yellow roller with huge yellow metal spikes angling out, now resting within the doorframe, & were quite shocked by it! A foreman on site with the crew, Dave Graham, came around and asked what had happened. He'd hired the steamroller, but he could hardly believe the damage it had done! We told him it was all right. It had been an honest mistake.

An enormous delivery was made of scads of drinks in paper sacks, probably consisting of slushies as well as perhaps meals. It was for the actors who would be rehearsing. This lot was accepted, brought in, and placed in a kayak at the top of the entrance to a long ramp of sharp descent.

Unfortunately, the kayak being plastic, it skittered down to the base of the ramp and into the water there, with all the other kayaks. Quite impossibly, its being plastic, it sank there.

We told Mum of all this. I'd learned I would have a primo role as the principal girl. I was all right with it, but not all that thrilled, as I'd played the role before. I later learned that the likely reason I'd been handed this choice role was tomfoolery that'd landed someone in a lot of hot water. Tricky, she, that 'someone', must have been. I had not detected so much as a blip on my radar.

I asked how soon the show would go up. 3 weeks. This was interesting! This shorter than normal time frame was why the earlier company had not got the job. Who would, then? A woman came in, & I blanched. Though highly regarded, I thought little of her loud, uncouth ways. She was the person who'd had drinks &/or food delivered.

Swimsuits and inner Silver Lining

At a swimming pool, we all wore skimpy swimwear. We were super young, and our bikinis and trunks complemented our bodies well. Although another girl had been designated to be my male friend's girl, I could tell he preferred me to her. It was a very innocent love. I was able to hang out for 10 to 12 hours without anyone minding.

One girl who I think was my friend's sister had to be checked urgently by an adult worker, probably a lifeguard. She opened her mouth very wide. We could all see intricate fanlike fleshy rows of plates lined up that made up her inner cheek linings. These plates were somewhat skinny, would slide over one another as she yawned wide to allow the mouth to open, and then retract back under as she closed her jaw. They had pretty, silver-striped markings on each groove. All our mouths had these.

There was a problem at the school in that there were not enough personnel to do formal observations on the faculty. So an alternative option was offered, & many had volunteered to go to a different school & have their assessments done while teaching different, older students unknown to them.

I had such trouble because my pants I'd donned had a little buckle on my right side that didn't fasten well. I showed my "busted" buckle to a pretty, thin, blonde-headed woman named Suzanne. She was middle-aged, as was I now. She knew the words to the song we'd all been trying to get all day, but none of us could remember them well. The song had a tune that we'd been humming at the pool, but we couldn't get the words right at the end. It was so tricky! She repeated it & helped me see where we'd been getting off on the lyrics.

I showed her the faulty buckle. It had finally stayed clasped for a little while, but I wasn't sure it was right. She looked, too, & we agreed. It must've been missing a part, possibly the little stem that would go through the hole & hold.

She asked if I knew two recruiters in the acting business. They were women. She tried describing one. A large woman who laughed a lot? She then showed me a picture from her wallet. The woman had a wide face with a big nose & mouth & big teeth. She was laughing very hard in the photo. "That's she!" I said. We both smiled and laughed. Not only did we both know this merry soul, I knew the other one, too.

I laughed again. I'd made a pretty good impression on her. Later I found that she is the very one doing observations at the other school with the different pupils.

Bus with Cinema

I was leaving a party where I'd had such fun with relatives I hadn't seen in many a year. I had been the life of the party.

I felt a bit ambivalent over the fact that I could now not recall to what extent I'd gone to provide everyone a good time. I didn't doubt that this was at least due in part to merrymaking activities I'd imbibed in. I seem to have seen clothes lying in a heap on the floor at one point. "Did I strip?" I asked myself. Oh, well. It was of no matter. At least it had been jolly good fun for all involved, I felt sure!

It was late, and the bus only stopped at certain stops on alternate routes. But I waited at the bus stop just in case it would pick me up. It stopped, and some kids got on.

I realised I was not supposed to ride this bus. I got on and hurried up the long staircase to the seating area, anyway. The man who was the driver was saying as I sat down that he had too many on and couldn't allow any more. The seats shifted. Somehow he'd missed seeing me, I felt sure. I was very relieved.

There were groupings of comfortable couches that ran parallel to the road as we drove and were away from the windows that were all shaded. It was very dim lighting. There was one main couch, and I sat on it with others my age. The driver walked along a huge screen before us because evidently the feature film would begin soon.

He pointed out something relative to the show we would view as he ran his hand along the screen. My emotions were confused. One second, fear at being discovered for being on this bus would override other feelings. The next, I was elated at being on this comfortable seat experiencing this interesting mode of transport. Alternatively, I worried that I would be found out at any moment for having gotten on too late, then glad about the upcoming movie, then scared I'd be caught for exceeding the maximum number of riders.

I later found out that some of the school busses were not going to be able to run at all on certain days. My former headmistress explained to my cousin who was a teacher that this would help her because on two days a week that she would have fewer students for whom to prepare lesson plans.

She would still have hundreds of students and assignments.

This same former superior told how they had ridden busses when she was a child with rigid plastic cases behind them. She laughed heartily at the thought. It wasn't clear whether the children sat with these as seat backs, or if they were early backpacks, or something else entirely.

Mexican messes

At my mum and dad's house, a few families from Mexico were visiting. I stopped by while my parents were out, and there were so many loud, active, happy children all talking at once, changing clothes and eating, that the whole wing of rooms where they were staying was a hubbub. Parents were patiently indulgent, and then they all left.

I looked about. Clothes lay on every surface. They'd mangled some hangers, so I tried to bend the wire back into shape a bit, lest they hurt themselves upon their return.

It was so unusual to have the house to myself, I hardly knew what to do. I played the piano, and then I found my uncle outside working on a project. He ran a shop with all kinds of rare antiques and the like. I decided to go check it out.

In this store with the atmosphere of an old general store, there were sights and smells from bygone days. I saw a glass case with one old cigarette in each compartment, with the tobacco open to the air. I thought it wouldn't stay fresh for very long like that, but realised if someone bought these, they wouldn't smoke them anyway. Their value lay in the cigarettes themselves.

I went to a campsite that was deserted, save for one woman. The Mexican families had been here while I was at the house and the antique shop, and now this area was demolished. There were very long tables with deep indentions in the worktops filled with open food containers and junk. Open plastic tubs had what looked like bright orange gel in them. I didn't know if it was edible jelly or hair gel. Lids were lying about, too, with the sticky substance on them.

The woman was stepping out of an open-air shower. She asked me if I saw one of these gel containers. I said I did. She asked me to bring her one, so I did. She had very pale white skin, dark hair, and a fairly nice face, though she didn't smile at all.

Gym @ Greengrocer's w/ Martial Arts Match

At a greengrocer's, a woman was singing loudly as she shopped. She was a great singer and she entertained people in this way every time. I had been alone in an aisle at the very back of the store before she came through. She got an item as she sang vociferously and then went off to another area. I reached into a huge vat that had many slices of watermelon in it. The melon was very ripe, to the point that it was barely connected to the rind, and was cut almost through the pulpy part. I got a piece and barely shook it, so that the red fleshy part came off of the rind in my hands. Oops! I smiled. Oh, well. Now I wouldn't have to pay the tare rate for the peel.

A handsome, younger man who I knew was in a gymnasium with an entrance opening onto this grocery aisle. We were glad to see one another, so I went into the gym with him. We had on ghees. I had taken martial arts years ago. He wanted to test me on my forms, so I tried to remember them, but I was very rusty. He continually anticipated where I would block and would attempt to strike me, so the moves had more meaning rather than just punching air, pretending to ward off enemies. We were very appreciative of one another to the point that we were getting turned on, but we'd never act on our desires.

At an outdoor area, an elevated glass cubicle had multiple sinks, one of which was filled with sauce, a thick, rich chocolate pud. There were big slabs of what looked like chocolate biscotti and a paddle that customers could spin. It was self-serve. An elderly German man was actively twirling the oversized chocolate biscuit he'd selected in this deliciousness. The sauce and all looked so appetizing!

I was going to buy a trifle. The ancient, hunched man who waited on me was also German, I feel sure, as were all the others in line behind me. We were more than likely in Germany. I paid with a coin, but was due some change. This was a laborious process. He had to look around behind his register and in other drawers in the vicinity in an attempt to find proper coinage to make change. The coins were visible, and they were old and crumbling. I mentioned that I thought sometime I'd like to buy the chocolate treat like I'd seen earlier, and this was met with many derisive, contemptible barks of laughter by the old guy, quite the character.

Public library with Organic Surprises

The trough over there has water that may be mouldering along with other stuff that's in it, such as plant matter and the body that's lying there. It's a rather old looking man's. Maybe he's alive, or not. But his brain is surely turning, it's beginning now to rot. Alternate version:

That trough over there
has some water mouldering
with other stuff, too,
such as icky plant matter.
The body in there,

with the webbing on its face.
Oldish looking man's.
Maybe he is still alive,
or possibly not.
His brain is surely turning,
beginning to rot.

At a library where we all work, some people have
funny ways. One man comes in for just a minute
every day and then goes back out to the car park,
only to return later. There's a woman very
knowledgeable about how everything must be done.
She's in charge of the area of musical instruments
and books.

I saw a lot of books that belonged on a shelf.
Needing to be put back, they were put away almost
instantly. My older son turned the rack on its end
and poured all the books in with one movement.
They each slid down from inside and rested on the
exact area sized and meant for that particular one.

A man who had gone to the college was back. He
and many others had come in altogether. The book
on the counter had not yet been officially returned.
He took it nonetheless. This was not protocol. So I
asked if I could go check it in, and he said, "No". I
saw that there was a very helpful key to the book
made of a long colourful piece of construction
paper. It could interpret the order and make sense of
the contents. It seems to be like many useful sticky
notes all made together and could adhere to all page
headings at once without harming its pages. I

showed it to him, but he did not accept the offer. He was looking at it with a female colleague silently now, I think.

The man who comes and leaves, to return again, came in from the car park as was his wont, returned much musical equipment and went back out. He must have changed clothes before coming in again. He had long, light brown hair.

I pulled out a bit of my poop when nobody was looking and hoped to just get a bit that was bugging me, but it was like white saltwater taffy. I pulled it as far as I could extend my arm, but it wouldn't snap. I wrapped it round my hand a bit and tugged and tugged more and more out. Someone was in the WC, so I wrapped it up in my hand and walked around to wait until it was no longer occupied, hoping sincerely no one would or had taken heed.

Snowy Western Region + Garage & Barn

I was in a car while my husband was driving me and our younger son around as it snowed pretty hard. The roads were getting covered. As it would drop to freezing, my husband observed the road conditions might call for schools to be out tomorrow. This would affect me and my son, since we were both teachers. It was so beautiful to ride along seeing how the blacktop would look shiny wet and then clean-looking, white buildup would appear around the edges where the drifts caught first.

Later I was at a huge Protestant church in the Western Region that I hadn't attended since I was a girl. I had a lot of letters in nice enclosed envelopes to turn in for distribution among the congregants. There was a spacious hall for fellowship because it was evening, so the main sanctuary would have no service that night. On a table I found dozens of similarly pre-addressed cards. Only names were printed on these. I sorted through them and saw one I thought intended for me, "Y". I opened it, since it wasn't sealed. But no, it wasn't for me. I put mine amongst the others.

An informal song began by choir members. There were several men on the far right who would dance out a little to our right by just stepping to the side as they performed. They would stop singing while men on the far left stepped to the left a few steps in like fashion, and eventually they drifted in together to sing as one. It was great to see young and old, black and white, enjoying themselves so obviously while entertaining so well.

I went to a house in the suburbs. Because I didn't live in this town, I hung out in a garage where a door had been left open. This was a very comfortable space. There was a long, low banque for seating and some small tables where one could set things. I had been here before and had come to think of it as "mine".

Today a middle-grade junior school boy came out and talked with me pleasantly. He was a bit on the chunky side and very polite. His mother glanced out through a window or screen door from what I took to be their kitchen. I saw her brow furrow slightly but could tell she was busy and very likely had a high level of trust for her son, so didn't come out to question me.

I needed to get moving. I had to go to my brother's place that was far away, and I'd never travelled there from here. I had my bag in which I'd collected (most of) my things. I walked toward the open door, telling the child I must be off. His older sister came out. I asked if they had the time. She directed us to a timepiece set high up on a shelf that had a round display that glowed red. It looked like the liquid-filled tube in a huge level to me, in the shape of an uppercase "I". "It has not been tuned right," she said. She grappled with the round knobs on the right and left, as one might use to tune a radio or work an etch-a-sketch, to no avail.

I remembered that I had set a few sticks on the small, round table and went back. I said, "I just need to retrieve some sticks." The boy and I looked, for at first glance it appeared nothing was there, but lo and behold, there they were. They were small twigs and were amongst the things on the low table.

Once outside, I heard the boy say his brother was home, and I was aware of a car having pulled up but

I wasn't interested in meeting another family member so didn't turn my head to see.

My mother walked up. She had driven here and asked what I was doing. I told her I was going to see my brother and was in a hurry since I had to get back within a few hours to go to work. She asked to come along, so I said, "Why not?"

We drove a ways, and I realised we were right at the farm where my good friend I'd not seen in forever worked. She and her husband had a great enterprise raising flowers for cut arrangements. I saw the barn. A man pulled up and parked his car on the street, too. He got out and asked if someone he needed to find worked there, but I told him I didn't know. as I hadn't been in ages. He also strode onto the premises.

I saw my dear girl, though she nor I were hardly girls any more, bounding along with her pretty, long, dirty-dishwater-blond hair and her great, gangly legs. She had pulled the bottom front of her white tee-shirt in through the hole in the front's top and yanked it down the middle to jack it up, as she'd been hot. I'd done this many a time. But she'd pulled it down in the front too hard, so the base of the shirt had risen much too high and her breasts were almost fully visible. Being well-endowed, her large nipples showed as she walked into the huge barn where her brother and many others were at work. I told her, "You need to pull your shirt down." My breasts were coincidentally exposed as well. But since my mammary glands are so much smaller than hers, it didn't really matter much, or AS much, I should say. I'd cover them up, anyway, I supposed.

Explosive Mishap

You had to pick an activity when I was at camp, so I chose basketball. No females had been allowed to play on this team but I got on the bus nonchalantly, being a young woman.

Later, I worked for this same shuttle enterprise. We shuffled school children around in school buses to basketball games and practices. There was a great abundance of these buses. One other assistant was on the bus as it drove. It was automated or perhaps a driver drove steadily on a straight road at a constant speed.

We had to shift buses that came up from behind, so they'd be in front of us as we rode. It was rather easy, as I had one of the newfangled gigantic, robotic hands. With one of these on my right hand, I'd grasp the bus behind us and set it up to pass us. I would hold it aloft and reach it around the right rear corner of our bus from behind, setting it into a position parallel to our bus on the right side, and releasing it. It was as if there were an invisible track, wind tunnel, or force field there. Once the bus was in place and released, it would thrust past our bus incredibly fast, freeing our effort to get the next bus in the queue from behind that needed to pass us.

I got another, set it to the right; a third, positioned it; a fourth, with no problem. But the buses were coming at me faster. The change in frequency must have got my rhythm off. I got the next bus, but did not put it around the side so that it was parallel, but at an intersecting angle. It directly rammed and crashed the side of our bus with a loud explosion of metal on metal as its gears ground and its tyres squealed and undoubtedly burst, if not bursting off altogether.

My assistant and I were shocked at this! After collecting our wits, we assessed the damage. It was not too bad. It wasn't as if this hadn't happened before, I learned with great relief!

Dinner Party Time

This couple consisted of a loud, large woman who was beautiful in her own way and her husband, a randy man who chased skirts and cheated so much that it must have been apparent to his wife, though she didn't let on. A young, pretty neighbor he had been sleeping with showed up at their dinner party in a dress that looked distinctly like a negligee, and her belly looked distinctly round. He noticed she was showing and made a face. I could tell from his expression, he was not going to own up to having fathered it just as her smitten face fell.

I got the meat roasting for their dinner party and set the timer that would end the process when it was done (the roast would be done, as would be the process). I left. I strolled through neighbourhood hills where abundant trees still held autumnal leaves of every splendid hue toward home, though it was pretty far. Dusk was gathering. I had to walk along the bridge over a river, so I really hustled lest it be dangerous, but no car came by at that time. Getting back into my area, I heard children's voices as they played games such as Star Trek 50th Anniversary Trivial Pursuit and University Challenge. The kids would be so much smarter once they were able to return to school.

I got home physically. The party I'd left was going on in my house. The woman of the couple came by me, stopped, stepped up to me, popped a thin cigarette in my mouth, lit it for me, and left the room. She called, and I answered the phone a moment later by looking up at it. She asked about the meat, and I told her it was due to be taken out now. It should be done.

I don't think it was done, however. It must not have cooked quickly enough, or the temp had been tampered with. No matter. She knew I'd fulfilled my end of the bargain before leaving.

The man of the house was pulling in financial favors right and left. He was telling of how he'd made more than anyone when he'd worked as a manager at FunMart, billions. He said he only lost out because the employees had all come after his job. His wife said he'd done fine, especially for not having gone to college.

Something Old, Someone New?

A building on campus had storage rooms so stuffed with so many sweets that never did anyone eat them all. Food was left sitting out indefinitely or put in overflowing bags to be disposed of overnight. One could go in there and get enough for an army, and nobody would notice nor mind, if they happened to see. They would likely thank you for taking the unhealthy, delicious treats.

A very close friend was preparing for his second wedding. There were good dishes being placed about. Leaf-soaked water with brown tinges crept under the posh flat's front door from the flooded landing. This happened nearly every time it rained. Its smell was not off-putting.

An attendee, also a close friend, had a machine to scientifically dispel this somewhat annoying water by blowing it with special hoses with brushy bristles on their ends. You replaced the brushes in their respective slots while it was still turned on, and you must place each with the bristly end facing a certain way. Even if you did it right, leafy smelling water would mist you.

The new bride had the same first name as the former wife of my friend, who was divorced. She was very nice and so extremely sweet and pretty.

She, this calm woman, and I found ourselves alone while folks went about the business of settling into their sleeping arrangements for this coming night. My dad, for example, found an enormous bowl filled with fresh fruit on top of the refrigerator and took it down. I made a comment to her about this, but realised she wouldn't catch my reference because it'd been only 'former wife with the same name' who'd known the inside story. She smiled at me demurely, charmingly, in an engaging way. She was the same wife, but no one knew it except her and me!

Maths Mayhem & Snowy obstacles

I was helping teach Year 2s. Teacher Meg asked if I could teach subtraction. She had coloured chits. They were to use them as coins, & they could never have enough without redistributing (?). I asked when. Probably "after lunch" . . . There was a small sheet of paper with examples, & we put it on top of a big filing cabinet. Another young female came to help. (I was also young.) I found a gold, double-crescent-shaped clip earring on the floor. A big man came in, too. An older boy, 10 or so, had profound problems - trying to bite down on things, but was doing well for himself, so a man was also observing him.

We took all the children out into the hall. It was time for me to teach the math lesson. I had been forming an impression of giving students the coloured circles & pre-testing knowledge of the worth of each coin. I would have them put their answer down & cover it with a hand, at which point all would reveal their work at once. (A problem was that kids might see others' answers that were not covered & cheat that way.) But now they were crowded in this hall with no desk space. I'd not brought the activity, as I'd thought "after lunch". I got permission to go get the supplies. They weren't there.

Now I was walking very far, following a male teacher who was asking what I thought about kids not getting to come to school for extended periods, due to snow.

It had snowed, & we were climbing over and around snow covered obstacles on the roadside, like stacks of bricks. I touched one & snow, or something, crumbled. I quickly picked it up, replaced it, & hurried to catch up.

"I don't think it was too bad to miss," I was saying. A car meanwhile pulled up with a primary school boy in its front passenger seat. The road it was driving on was totally snow covered, while many (most), roads were clear. We were working for a school system in a remote area.

I realised I would get paid & was now a teacher. I think I was getting full teacher's pay, though I was more or less an aide, because the system had the funding budgeted. So they thought, "Why not?"

I wondered if former fellow teachers would know I'd found work. I assumed not, since I was physically remote. But I thought that if they knew, they'd be proud.

Baby w/ Tree - a new Family

A man raising the infant alone was in over his head. I, a single woman, took the baby in, and met no quarrel over it. After a few weeks, the little one and I were faring well. It was fine with me that this fellow hadn't come round to inquire.

I went to see a woman who worked at the little shop with the biological father. Earlier, she had stopped in, checking to see how we were.

The babe was still flourishing, and we were knitting together a solid bond, so it was settled that I would in fact live with and raise the child for the foreseeable future. No clothing to speak of for the tyke had come in the bargain, but a rare, twining tree had. In just a few weeks span, it had grown up the blank wall, arced, and now had descended again. I'd reinforced it by securing it to the wall at that sloping juncture. Its trunk had bulked out to be quite large. I thought it was branching off, parallel to the flat's floor. I hoped so.

While at the shop, I asked the woman again about the solicitor she'd mentioned to me. She assured me that he was a good one, housed in the same strip of businesses. He would do nicely for what I was needing. There was a public loo I entered while getting up my nerve to make this guardianship official. A full length looking glass showed my beige dress slacks to be even longer than I thought they were. I was wearing a pair of 5" vintage brown leather stacks from the '70s. The pants completely covered these and trailed behind me a foot or so. I turnt to peer back at my reflection. I could see that the effect was oddly striking, but not in a good way.

I met the lawyer. We basically scheduled an appointment to discuss the matter of the child at a later date. He took me in with his eyes, and said with an ingratiating look, not too disapprovingly, "You should get yourself some different clothes."

"I didn't know if there were clothing shops in the area," I said, in an inquiring way.

"There are some that would suit you, but you have to drive to the city. It's not far." I decided this would be a fine idea. As the baby had just the one outfit, I'd buy new things for her, too.

Squatting for No Reason

I was squatting in a house in a foreign country where an ex of mine was staying for an extended time with his current wife and brother. They were here on holiday. It was difficult to conceal my presence, so I took every pain to cover my tracks.

One day, I crossed the road to the huge body of water nestling there amidst the mountains. It was vibrant blue, and its waters that rippled in the nippy wind were pristine. I made my way out onto a small promontory of large blue-grey rocks and boulders and flung the contents of my bladder and bowels into the lake. I stooped to swish out the pot a little, as some bits hadn't flung out quite. I was observed by the brother of my ex. So my gig was up.

Later, I found that my presence was not a matter of contention, nor even of much interest or consequence. They seemed to be so matter-of-fact about it as to be rather dull, hardly conversing amongst themselves about any matters of existence whatsoever. So I could stay on, and nothing was made of it.

One (or Two) in Every Bunch

All of us teachers were sitting for an exam. It was top priority, and I was responsible for security, along with a colleague. It was, of course, timed. I sat at a huge round table. I left after a couple of minutes because, despite being tested, I had other things to attend to.

I went down the hall to the home area of the school. I had to take a shower. Once this important business was conducted, I ate a little and then made my way back in. Granted, I would have to complete my test in less time.

A woman sitting to my left was talking aloud to the woman sitting to her left. I immediately told her there was no talking. This had been made explicit when I'd earlier read the testing rules and parameters aloud. They carried on a running convo, and they were collaborating over the questions. I repeated, "NO talking!" It continued. I looked around for my co-administrator. She was at a table somewhat distant, but doubtless had to have heard every word. Maybe she could tune it out, being somewhat removed. I was livid at the talking women and at my helper.

There was a problem with the testing, and it was halted. Every teacher exited the building, ambling along, due to the large number of testing rooms emptying into the hallways. I saw a pretty baby in a stroller look up at me in wonder as she was pushed slowly through the crowd. How sweet were her searching eyes, so innocent and immune to the hatred I was feeling.

Expansive Experiences

We were driving through a neighbourhood in a desert. My husband was at the wheel. A very large lorry with its original tyres having been replaced by hugely oversized versions roared loudly down and away from us through a wide alleyway behind a house. I guess it was an alley, but on one side was nothing, save a great expanse of sand. The truck was so loud. It seemed a menacing, aggressive presence. My husband said we were the outsiders here, after all, insinuating these scofflaws could do as they pleased by driving like hellions every day here, and it was none of our concern.

We came to a dead end. On the right, a backyard garden was a marvel to behold. The structure was a low, one-level ranch house. Some high reaching trees cast shadow. Plants here below had curving forms that sought to defy description, so varied and unusual were they. Having traveled halfway around the world, I'd not seen any of these species. Perhaps they were cacti or varietal hybrids. Though shaded, sunlight (rays? particle?) beams filtered down through the lofty branches. The effect lit up the dazzlingly colourful plants to clearly display each hue.

Panning my head to the left, the garden opposite this bounteous feast for the eyes was nice, neat, and trim. "I want to live here," I said to my husband with a wonderful tone, gesturing back toward our right.

We got turned about and were leaving the area, but both were drawn to one home on the left of the deserted desert street. A middle-aged woman, with long, black hair worn lax, was in the front garden. It was apparent that she was one who clearly had mysterious properties of unseen attraction. Both my mate and I felt her draw. He stopped the lorry. Being the highly cynical beings we are, we nonetheless got out and walked slowly to her.

She was as unfazed in all of this as one could get.
She said we should come on inside, she was 'glad
we could make it.' She'd fetch the size shoes my
husband's feet were wanting. When she came back
with a shoebox, I looked at her own footwear. One
of her soft moccasins came off, and so delicately
thin and well-worn it was! I saw, rather than felt,
that I now had the moc on my foot. It fitted exactly,
wrapping and swaddling my foot, so that I wanted
never to remove it.

Over and Out

There were hordes of people everywhere you
looked, on every tier of the circular proscenium.
Gathering here, this was their Mecca. It was
exceedingly difficult if not impossible to move up
one step, over a step on the level I was on, or down.
I found myself wondering what I was doing here.

This was all wrong. I had made a grave mistake. I
had to get out posthaste.

Without actually having room for such a maneuver,
I did a back walkover. I found I was standing on the
large oval of paper that could enable my escape if I
could manage the act properly. I knew it had to start
on one part of the oval, and possibly overlap down a
step, if this was to work. The landing had to stick,
though! I saw no other choice. Really.

I nailed it! Well, it may have garnered a 1 or 2 in the Olympic Games, if that. But for my age, wow! I was out, and that was all I cared about!

Betrayal

One had to be fitted with leg-warmer type casts/legwear/leg ware. To walk in snow, the two parts had to overlap. There was a space that <u>had</u> to be doubled. (This was due to COVID-19.) I refused to wear it, this legware.

At work, a woman who'd been hired wondered if she would be formally observed. She asked me about it, and I told her that she knew she would have to be. I was to set up employees' cars in the car park with tracking devices. The new employee saw me throwing away parts that I would need in order to set up the devices.

Other workers were there, setting up for a meal, and they probably saw me toss the parts, too. I had tried to put spy equipment on 1 car. I'd gone back and gotten the spyware out, however. The headmistress had told me to install it. She talked to me while I discarded the pertinent hardware, but she never noticed.